EXPOSURE

EXPOSURE

Two Plays by Greg MacArthur

Coach House Books

first edition

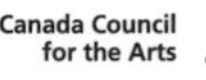

Published with the assistance of the Canada Council for the Arts and the Ontario Arts Council. We also acknowledge the Government of Ontario through the Ontario Book Publishing Tax Credit Program and the Government of Canada through the Book Publishing Industry Development Program.

LIBRARY AND ARCHIVES CANADA CATALOGUING IN PUBLICATION

MacArthur, Greg, 1970-
Exposure : two plays / Greg MacArthur. – 1st ed.

Complete contents: Snowman – Girls! girls! girls!.
ISBN 1-55245-155-0

I. Title. II. Title: Snowman. III. Title: Girls! girls! girls!.

PS8625.A78E96 2005 C812'.6 C2005-901761-9

CONTENTS

Violence, Youth and Rites of Passage: An introduction by Peter Hinton

Recently, an American survey was conducted on teens and violence. By apt coincidence (funny, I am sure, to the playwright), it was called the MacArthur Violence Risk Assessment Program – named after a different MacArthur, but interested in the same social phenomena. A test group of teenagers was asked to report on violence that had occurred in the previous month, while another group was asked to report on violence in the previous year. The teenagers who reported on violence in the previous year should have reported about twelve times as much violence as the one-month group; however, the two groups reported roughly the same amount. While it was clear that the students in the one-month group weren't actually more violent and that the study didn't ask about one particularly violent month, the study's authors determined that the experience was perceived as the same. The authors suggested that teens weren't deliberately lying; because memory doesn't record numbers of things specifically, the experience was perceived as the same.

No matter how the subject has been examined, violence appears to be a fact of life for most teenagers. And in the plays of Greg MacArthur, violence is not an isolated action that threatens societal norms but rather the very condition by which characters understand and define themselves. In the study, almost all teenagers reported both committing and being the victim of some form of violence, although most said that this violence did not cause serious injury. The survey concluded that violence (as well as a reputation for it) serves special functions in the lives of young people. It is used to acquire and maintain status; kids who are known to be tough, fearless and able to fight achieve status among their peers. Being afraid lowers status. So teens are often motivated to enhance their own reputation for toughness by overreporting the fear and injury they cause to others and underreporting what they experience.

What is paradoxical is that, far from bestowing status, violence towards another is, in our larger culture, something one is expected to feel ashamed of; however, the desire to keep it secret is so strong that many rationalize it to the point that they don't even consider their actions violent in the first place. This is the pertinent and troubled terrain of Greg MacArthur's theatre.

girls! girls! girls! was written in response to the 1999 Columbine High School massacre, in which two seventeen-year-old boys, Eric Harris and Dylan Klebold, killed twelve students and a teacher before committing suicide. At that time, MacArthur was following very closely the trials of the Reena Virk murder case, in which a fourteen-year-old girl was brutally beaten and subsequently drowned in Victoria, British Columbia.

As MacArthur began work, he was moved not only by the terror struck into the lives of the victims but also by the unrecognized struggles of the killers – the distorted yet human face of social rebellion and boredom, recklessness and control.

Far from being a social-issue docudrama, *girls! girls! girls!* is a poetic tragedy that examines the degrees by which violence can occur and the socially enforced regulation of behaviour and desensitization to experience. Written in a hip-hop nursery-rhyme language, it shows five teenagers attempting to demonstrate individual power and giving a voice to private pain, all in the context of a strict and regimented social group. The language, made up almost entirely of borrowed phrases and imagery from television, pop culture and film, seduces the speaker into believing that images are preferable to experience. The dialogue is written almost entirely in the third person, creating a theatrical way of speaking that defiantly allows a character to express herself, while at the same time remaining personally absent and removed. It is a language that both negates and defines the speaker. This high presentational style is contrasted with a lean and economical realist narrative: MacArthur focuses his characters around the pressures of an amateur gymnastics competition. The action of each scene is brutally sparse, driven by events that explore the gloating of the winner and the revenge of the girl who lost: a series of sixteen minimalist vignettes with short blasts of pop music and lush soliloquies in between.

Despite the heavy stylization, MacArthur always manages to get inside the heads of his characters. Whether in the rough punk third person or in frank and personal prose, the writing is generally cool, but always in a strange and animated way. The result is unsettling, unique and ruthlessly unsentimental. The play does not answer questions; instead, it is a crude denouncement of reckless emotion and a chronicle of the lives of the unrewarded. In *girls! girls! girls!* we feel for the young killers as the inevitable result of a society that both worships and devours its young.

In startling contrast, *Snowman* is a much more subtle and poetic work. It is a play about entering adulthood. Set on the edge of a glacial sheet, it depicts this landscape as a habit of mind. Here MacArthur examines the lives of four slightly older people who feel they are on the verge of extinction. All of them are drifters, running from an unresolved past or abandoned to forge a new life alone. Part horror show, part post-modern confessional, it is a play that captures the psychology of desire and hopelessness, passion and frigidity, cohesion and detachment.

For the Whitehorse production in 2004, MacArthur wrote, 'Although this play was originally inspired by the discovery of the "iceman" near Haines Junction a number of years ago, it was not meant to be a factual recreation of the events surrounding this discovery. Rather, that event became the basis for my own journey – my story – of escape and discovery. A majority of this play was written over the course of one frosty winter in Montreal. I had just moved to *la belle province* from my home in Toronto, hoping to escape some demons and hoping to find some peace. Holed up in a strange city, alone, the image of that lost boy, frozen into the ice, kept haunting me. More and more, I became immersed in his strange imagined world – a world of frozen people, stuck at the edge of nowhere. Like the characters in this play, I've spent most of my life running ... running from something, running to something. Hoping to find my own snowman. Hoping to have the courage to dig him out of the ice. Hoping to face him.'

In the play, Denver and Marjorie are a couple who periodically, and for no concrete reason, pack up their lives and move to another town. It is an apt example of life in transition, both running away from encumbrances of a probably conventional life and holding on to a youthful ideal or sense of possibility, of adventure. Beautiful but vacant, possibly pathological, an abandoned local, Jude, is 'adopted' by Denver and Marjorie when he comes looking for gay porn by the video rental store they run out of their home. The discovery of a prehistoric man, entombed in the ice sheet, spears through the emotional stasis of each character's life, forcing them to confront the pasts they have suppressed within the chilling isolation of their northern environment. Something in the stark loneliness of the body enthralls each character's imagination, thrusting them into deep personal examination. With each character metaphorically frozen, the snowman's gradual thawing and decomposing in the sun parallels their own emergence from a state of denial and apathy.

Language in MacArthur's text often serves as a social mask that each character manipulates or struggles against. Puss and Jam, the leaders of the gang in *girls!*, wear extreme white face and heavy black eyeliner, on one hand resembling typical Goth teens but on the other hand transforming them into warriors from an imagined Kabuki epic. Little Bucky becomes increasingly bloody and covered in mud as the play progresses, reflecting both the realism of the beatings he endures but also the shift in his psychology. By the time he is reunited with the girls, he resembles an almost primitive man of earth and flesh (curiously, not unlike Jude's decomposing snowman), a far cry from the socially cynical construct we meet in the first scene. In *Snowman*, Marjorie discovers the infidelity between Denver and Kim when she sees them dressed in identical matching snowsuits. Fully concealed with black balaclavas, Kim and Denver resemble aliens more than lovers: comic and horrific, like characters from the videos Denver emulates. The exterior mask reveals the interior reality. The characters most victimized, or, rather, the characters that appear as 'outsiders' in the plays (Missy in *girls!* and Kim in *Snowman*) appear to wear no masks at all, although Missy is marked by her red ribbon and Kim is distinguished by her emblem of middle-class achievement: a briefcase.

Both plays explore self-defined rites of passage, moving from the idealism of childhood to the compromised paradox of adult life: a journey that contrasts private experience with social definition. Adulthood in MacArthur's drama is a construct – of social and sexual regulation but also of hypocrisy. The so-called 'real' world his characters rebel against and must ultimately submit to is one based on the perpetuation of secrets and abuse – an unreal world to his protagonists, who prefer a world of zombie and slasher films, which to them more accurately reflect the world they face.

In many respects these plays expose the most existential aspects of adolescence and the disconnection and rage that lie beneath the surface of middle-class values. Indeed, the schoolyard and forested ravine of *girls!* or the glacial field and the homey description of Jude's kitchen in *Snowman* are hardly the environments of murder, revenge and decomposing body parts. However, the natural world proves to be a poetic landscape in which MacArthur's powerless and neglected protagonists can at last emerge and reclaim who they are. Ultimately, these plays are tragedies of Greek proportion, told through the modern Canadian experience. While many see Canada as a model of openness, tolerance and generosity, a country of perseverance and progress, these are perhaps nothing but clichés about our national character. MacArthur is anything but exclusively inward-looking, timid and anonymous. His plays pose questions about what our true nature might become: conflicted, restless and accountable. Reminding us we are transformed, for better or worse, by every experience.

I first met Greg MacArthur when he was training as an actor at the Ryerson Theatre School in Toronto. Curious, demanding, particular and peculiar: MacArthur was unforgettable. I think his essence as an actor is best expressed in these plays. They are texts that, as well as having literary merit, are first and foremost meant to be spoken aloud. Over the years we remained in contact, and I remember reading an early play entitled *The Rise and Fall of Peter Gaveston*, a contemporary deconstruction of Marlowe's *Edward II*, nine years ago. Heavily influenced by Howard Barker, Sarah Kane and the British Royal Court Writers, Greg's theatrical and intellectual imagination was inspired. Somewhat lost, I think, in a Canadian theatre practice steeped in confessional and poetic naturalism, his work has always been difficult to define, and, until recently, too nerve-wracking for theatres to consider for production. Largely supported through David Oiye, Artistic Director of Toronto's Buddies in Bad Times, MacArthur is the self-described Rhubarb! alumnus of all time. He sent a script to me five years ago when I was working as Dramaturge at Playwrights' Workshop Montreal. The first draft of *girls! girls! girls!* leapt off the page and grabbed the actors (gathered round a table for an informal reading) by the throat. Since then, I have had the great pleasure of directing two productions of *girls!* and the Montreal premiere of *Snowman* in 2004. Without question, I think MacArthur is one of the most vital, relevant and exploratory playwrights working in English Canada today. *Snowman* and *girls! girls! girls!* mark the beginning of MacArthur's mature work. He has left his mentors behind and is writing in a truly authentic and unique voice. At the time of this publication, *Snowman* will have received four productions in Canada, and his newest play *Get Away* will have premiered at the Alberta Theatre Projects. Things are changing for MacArthur, and one can only hope, as one must always do, to ensure the continuity and growth of any artist struggling to survive in the marginalized, disparate world of Canadian theatre, that the best of Greg MacArthur is yet to come.

SNOWMAN

Snowman was first produced by Section 8 Theatre (presented by Rumble Productions) in Vancouver, British Columbia, in April 2003.

Denver: Derek Metz
Jude: Kevin MacDonald
Marjorie: Jody-Kay Marklew
Kim: Erin Monahan

Directed by Craig Hall
Set and costume design by Craig Hall, Kevin MacDonald and Yvan Morisette
Lighting design by Yvan Morisette
Sound design by Robert Perrault

It has subsequently been produced at the Baxter Theatre Centre (Cape Town, South Africa), Imago Theatre (Montreal, Quebec), Buddies in Bad Times Theatre (Toronto, Ontario) and Nakai Theatre (Whitehorse, Yukon).

Snowman was written and developed with the assistance of the Canada Council for the Arts, Playwrights' Workshop Montreal, Buddies in Bad Times Theatre's 2002 Rhubarb! Festival, the National Arts Centre's On the Verge ... Festival of New Work, and the 2002 Banff playRites Colony (a partnership between the Canada Council for the Arts, the Banff Centre for the Arts and Alberta Theatre Projects).

My thanks to the following for their inspiration, encouragement and support in development of this script: Peter Hinton, Paula Danckert, David Oiye, Craig Hall, Kevin MacDonald, Lise Ann Johnson, Michael Clarke, Peter and Sandy MacArthur and the many actors across the country who gave these characters a voice and a heart.

This play is for Sionnach.

CHARACTERS

DENVER
a man in his mid-thirties, a little past his prime

JUDE
a nineteen-year-old boy, solitary and beautiful

MARJORIE
a woman in her mid-thirties, a little past her prime

KIM
a woman in her thirties, an archaeologist

PRODUCTION NOTES

This play takes place in a small community at the edge of a glacial sheet. No effort should be made to realistically portray this.

Movement and the use of props should be concise and minimal.

PART ONE

SCENE ONE

DENVER: *(to audience)* We live simple and quiet, me and Marjorie. We got what we need and we like what we got. Not much. A wood stove, a Ski-Doo, a collection of videos.

I always thought I was the kind of person who needed more from life. I was wrong.

I'm not afraid to change my opinion of myself. People tend to get an idea of themselves and generally stick with it. For fear of being contradictory.

Like my dad. He was a bastard. Always was. Couldn't seem to shake it. When I was a kid he made me cry all the time.

One day he said – my mom was downstairs writing Christmas cards – he said, 'Get the fuck out of my house.'

I left big snowy footprints in the driveway.

I went to a nearby city. I worked at a video store and met Marjorie at a booze can. She was fucking ripped. We did some speed she had in her purse.

For a while I was happy. Then I wasn't.

Marjorie said, 'Pick a direction and let's go.'

North seemed good. I never had a problem with cold. Some people do. Not me. I'm warm-blooded.

Or is it cold-blooded? I could never keep that fact of science straight.

(pause)

Fuck it.

I stole seven boxes of videotapes from the store and loaded them into our car. New releases, classics, some porn.

We took off.

We'd drive till we hit a place we both liked. Rent an apartment, get jobs, walk around, make friends.

Sometimes we'd stay a month. Sometimes a year. Depended on the job. Depended on the friends.

When the time came, we'd just pack up the car and that was that.

We've been doing this for about ten years. Going north.

We currently live in a spit of a town at the edge of a glacial sheet. Go past that row of trees and it's ice. Go past the ice and it's ice. You get the idea.

We rent videos out of our house. I cut wood for people and generally fuck around. We scrape by.

Our friend Jude says we're lucky we got each other.

Jude's a piece. Messy hair and big eyes. Wears gumboots and a big toque and pulls it off. He's got this ... magnetic appeal. You can't stop looking at him. In the city he'd be the cat's meow. Beautiful people'd want to hang with him. Here he's just –

JUDE: I hear you have some videos to rent.

DENVER: I do.

JUDE: I wouldn't mind seeing one.

DENVER: You got any particular tastes?

JUDE: I don't know.

DENVER: We got a catalogue. Marjorie made it. She lives here. It's not much, but it's alphabetized. You can browse through it.

JUDE: You have any recommendations?

DENVER: I wouldn't want to be – what's the word? – presumptuous.

(pause)

JUDE: Maybe some porn.

DENVER: You want some porn?

JUDE: If you got any.

DENVER: Well. I got some porn.

JUDE: Can I see what you got?

DENVER: What do you like?

JUDE: Guys.

DENVER: Now we're getting specific. Now we're getting down to the nitty-gritty. Now I can help you.

(pause)

JUDE: This looks good.

DENVER: It's German.

JUDE: You need to see any ID? I got a card here with my name on it.

DENVER: You seem like a straight-up guy.

JUDE: Well, I don't like to cause trouble or cheat people.

DENVER: I don't expect you do.

(pause)

JUDE: Um ... I don't have a TV or VCR. I'm not really hooked up to anything.

DENVER: We got a good system in our living room. Me and Marjorie. You wanna come in and watch it here?

JUDE: Thanks.

DENVER: *(to audience)* His parents bailed on him years ago. He was just a kid. Woke up one morning expecting eggs and bacon and got slapped with a bye-bye note saying, 'We're gone kiddo. Sorry 'bout the mess.'

Maybe they looked at their kid sleeping and couldn't bear it. Maybe they got scared of what they saw in him. Or maybe they were just bastards.

Jude's got this idea they got so cold and frosty their hearts froze up. They left to find the sun. They're travelling around looking to be warm and they're gonna come back for him.

I don't know. I don't know. Anything's possible. I live next to a glacier renting porn tapes to teenagers and I'm happy.

Anything's possible.

(Marjorie turns to Jude.)

MARJORIE: Who's this?

DENVER: He's got no TV, so –

MARJORIE: What's his name?

JUDE: Jude.

(pause)

MARJORIE: Jude. Wouldn't you rather be doing this somewhere else?

JUDE: I got no TV.

DENVER: He's got no TV.

MARJORIE: He's got no TV.

(pause)

MARJORIE: Maybe we should leave him alone.

JUDE: I don't mind the company.

DENVER: He don't mind.

MARJORIE: He don't mind.

(pause)

DENVER: *(to audience)* So, Jude comes over every now and then. We get to know him. We go through all the German gay pornography we got. Some tapes we watch twice. Jude brings some coke over the odd time and we have a real party.

Coke's easy to get up here. Can't get a chunk of feta cheese to save your life, but coke – they fly it in, cut it up, fly it out. We get the runoff.

Marjorie warms up to him over time. Takes a real shine to him, my mom would say.

I liked him the moment I saw him.

Those big eyes.

Something ... the way he looks at me ... it makes me want to take care of him.

JUDE: I'm going out on the glacier. Look at the lights. Build a snowman.

DENVER: We're gonna put on a horror. *Invasion of the Body Snatchers*, maybe. We're gonna stay in and get scared.

(pause)

DENVER: Maybe *Nightmare on Elm Street*.

(pause)

JUDE: You guys are lucky you got each other.

DENVER: *(to audience)* Jude disappears on the glacier all the time. Spends hours by himself. I don't know what he does out there. Building snowmen, I guess. There ought to be about a thousand of them by now.

Marjorie says they're gonna rise up, march into town and gun us down one of these days. Jude and his army of snowmen. They're gonna massacre the whole lot of us. That's what Marjorie says.

Man. Fucking *Children of the Corn*. Creepy.

I'm thinking, though, us being Jude's friends and all, I'm thinking we'll be spared. If the snowmen go berzerk. We'll be spared.

SCENE TWO

JUDE: (*to audience*) The night my parents left, I heard the car pull out of the driveway. I got up and went to the kitchen window.

The car stalled halfway down the driveway, stuck on a patch of ice.

Mom sat in the car.

I was at the window.

She put her gloves on. She got out and helped Dad push the car.

I was at the window. I watched them struggle.

At one point, Mom slipped and banged her chin on the fender. Dad grabbed a handful of snow and iced it. For the swelling, I guess.

It took about twenty minutes for them to get unstuck.

I thought I should go out and help them. I thought I would just get in the way.

They finally got the car onto the main road.

I went back to bed.

SCENE THREE

MARJORIE: (*to audience*) He said, 'Let's go north.'

What did I know? I worked at a restaurant that served bad food. I was greasy all the time. North seemed like a real step up.

When you don't know what you want and someone offers you something, you generally jump at it.

Denver's got an easy disposition. What I mean is, he goes with things. He's easy that way.

Me? I don't know. I walk around this place and I literally bump into things. I go outside and I don't know where I'm going. I'm cold all the time.

I keep things inside me till I forget they're there.

I have very few memories of my life when I was young. I remember being fourteen and feeling sad because this guy told me I was ugly. Everything before that is a total haze. I'm not exaggerating.

Sometimes I sit in a chair frozen solid. I have this idea someone is gonna come and excavate me. A long cut down my belly. Reach down and dig in deep. Bring things up and out of me.

They'll put what they find inside me on the floor and I'll go through it. Words, faces, expressions, thoughts. All covered in blood and bile. I'll pick them up and clean them and arrange them in a circle around me.

Denver will come in and he'll see me. He'll stand over me, looking down. Kind of disgusted and terrified all at once. He won't know what to say.

DENVER: *(to Marjorie)* Me and Jude are gonna go hit some golf balls out on the glacier.

MARJORIE: (*to audience*) I told Jude about my fantasy. I thought he might have something to say. Some kind of insight. He's got a unique way of looking at things. He can appreciate honest feelings.

He told me he thought that was fucked up.

We watched some porn on the TV.

SCENE FOUR

JUDE: (*to audience*) Denver and Marjorie.

I don't know.

The thing is, they're always acting like they're helping me out just by spending time with me, you know?

Like they're doing me a mammoth favour by inviting me over and talking to me about things.

They'll say, 'Jude, come over, we'll have some homemade pizza.' Like that's gonna be some kind of fantastic, mind-blowing thrill for me. Like I've been waiting my whole life for them to show up and entertain me.

The thing is, I find Denver sexy. I like being around him and looking at him. He turns me on. And that's about the end of it. I'm really a shallow person.

If Denver got maimed somehow or lost his appeal, I don't think I would give a shit about him.

When we watch porn together, I think about him.

Marjorie is okay, but when we're alone she's got this thing about talking incessantly about psychotic shit and these deep personal dilemmas of hers.

I don't know.

Like because my parents took off and I'm quiet and like German porn that somehow makes me interested in the human psyche.

People get abandoned all the time. It doesn't make them anything.

Denver and Marjorie are lonely people. All they have is each other. That kind of dependency gives me the creeps. I find it pathetic.

Denver comes over and says, 'Let's go hit some golf balls out on the glacier.'

What the hell. I suppose there's worse ways to spend your time. Like sitting at home dreaming about being carved up 'cause you have no memory of yourself.

I'm thinking about that when I bend down to pick up an orange golf ball.

That's when I see him.

I see his arm. I see his fingers. Sticking out of the ice beside a rock. The sun blistering them ... cooking them.

I see his body, curled up, naked, frozen under the ice.

I see his face, open, lost.

The first thing I thought, the first thing I thought when I saw him was, he's mine. He was a secret I wanted to keep.

I leave the orange golf ball beside his arm to mark the spot. I don't say anything to Denver.

That night in bed I feel this hand reach up and touch me.

SCENE FIVE

DENVER: (*to audience*) I tell Marjorie we're expanding our video operation. We're getting into games, I tell her. Nintendo, PlayStations, Game Boys, all that shit. Three smartass teenagers came in asking.

In a place this size, that's a major customer demand. That's a call to arms.

One of them, short and stocky. Squinty eyes. Muscular. Shaved head. Uneven, like he did it himself in a dirty mirror. The bulldog.

'Where's your games? You got any games?'

I said, 'What games?'

He said, 'Nintendo, shithead.'

I wanted to slap him. I don't like being out of touch.

The other two. Rasta boys. Brothers maybe. Same sneakers, same toques, same age. White dreadlocks hanging over their eyes. Bob Marley's face on their sleeves.

They look down at the ground and spit. I look at their saliva sitting there on my wood floor.

'Next week,' I said.

So, we're expanding our video operation, I tell Marjorie. Nintendo games, some new releases –

MARJORIE: We're out of kindling.

DENVER: (*to audience*) I think about going to see Jude. I'd like to hear a supportive voice. I haven't seen him in a while. He's been scarce.

MARJORIE: Denver, we're out of kindling.

DENVER: Yeah – What are you saying, Marjorie?

MARJORIE: We're out of kindling.

DENVER: (*to audience*) Jesus. One day you're out in the snow and sun having a blast with a nine iron. The next day your girl's laying in on you and your friend's scarce.

I don't like that.

(*to Marjorie*) You seen Jude lately?

MARJORIE: No.

DENVER: Hm.

MARJORIE: (*to audience*) Nintendo, he says. All of a sudden I feel sick when I look at him. Accidents happen with axes, I think to myself.

DENVER: Maybe we should get some more porn. While we're at it. While we're getting the Nintendo. We should get some more porn.

SCENE SIX

JUDE: (*to audience*) My snowman.

I lie in bed all day and think about him. I don't answer the phone. I don't answer the door.

I sink myself into a bathtub full of water. I lie there for hours, in the dark, in the bathtub, the water cold and murky, and I imagine him.

Where he came from. His life. His name.

Every night I gear myself up for my expedition.

I start to get a little paranoid. I take a different route each time to cover my tracks. Sometimes I think I'm being followed. I start carrying a knife with me.

At first, I just sit there looking at him.

His hands … his fingers … the ones poking through the ice are not in good shape. They're starting to turn. They're going off. From exposure, I guess.

I think about cutting them off with my knife.

But then I think, what would I do with them?

I reach into my pocket. I've got a freezer bag with some sliced carrots. I finish off the carrots. I lay the freezer bag on the ice.

I sit there and look at him.

DENVER: Marjorie?

JUDE: (*to audience*) I think about Marjorie and her fucked-up fantasy. All that stuff rotting inside of her.

DENVER: I gonna talk to Mrs. Cran at the library. See if I can use her computer system. She's hooked up to the Internet. You can order pretty much anything you want and they deliver it to you. They mail it out to you.

Marjorie?

JUDE: (*to audience*) I move closer to him. I brush the snow away to get a better look at his face. I lie down on top of him.

DENVER: I'm gonna get them their fucking Nintendo. If they come by, you tell them that. Those teenage shitheads.

Marjorie?

Marjorie?

JUDE: (*to audience*) On the ice. We're face to face. Me and him.

MARJORIE: Jude?

JUDE: (*to audience*) I take out my knife.

SCENE SEVEN

DENVER: (*to audience*) Marjorie gets like this sometimes. Fucking zombies out. Sits there like the world is over. Throw something at her, she wouldn't blink.

What am I supposed to do with that? I leave.

It takes me about twenty minutes to get to Jude's house. I speed walk across the gravel. I work up a sweat. Stars are dancing above me. I don't look up once.

It's got a real rustic charm to it, Jude's house. Lots of wallpaper and furniture. A kitchen full of pots and pans. You can see a family living here. You can see them being comfortable.

I think about the morning his parents left. I think about Jude waking up, rubbing his eyes, in his pyjamas, walking around, lost. I wonder where they left the goodbye note. I think maybe on the fridge.

It's strange to be in someone's house when they're not there. It's uncomfortable.

I look through the closets. I open up the cupboards. Killing time. I sit there in the dark at the kitchen table.

It's gotta be about eleven by now. Those damn teenagers. I can hear their snotty voices. Like I'm some loser video store clerk and they're a bunch of gangsters.

I get this urge to go find them and beat the shit out of them.

I decide to wait for Jude. Maybe he'd want to come and watch.

I take my sweater off. Dry it off by the stove. I sit there in my T-shirt.

In Jude's house.

JUDE: Hey.

DENVER: Hey.

JUDE: Jesus –

DENVER: I let myself in.

(pause)

I just been sitting here.

(pause)

You been scarce lately. What's up?

JUDE: (*to audience*) Jesus. I'm cold and paranoid. I come home and want to climb into bed. I want to be alone. And there's Denver, sitting at the kitchen table. It's dark and he's wearing a T-shirt.

DENVER: Got yourself a new boyfriend?

JUDE: Yeah, that's right. A real stud. German porn star named Ivan. Bumped into him at the Quick Stop convenience store.

(*to audience*) Boyfriend? What the hell is he talking about?

DENVER: You just gonna leave him out there in the cold?

JUDE: (*to audience*) He's looking at me like he really wants something. You don't climb into someone's empty house and sit there in the dark in a T-shirt if you don't.

DENVER: Jude?

JUDE: I get an erection.

DENVER: I'm thinking about getting into Nintendo.

JUDE: What?

DENVER: Nintendo games, video games. What do you think about that?

JUDE: I don't know.

DENVER: Expand the operation. Branch out. I'm gonna order it off the Internet.

JUDE: (*to audience*) He leans forward in his chair. His hands spread out on the kitchen table. I look at his fingers, big and rough, twitching.

My snowman. His fingers, dead and black in my pocket

I sit down on a chair across from Denver. He's sweating a bit. My heart is racing.

My knife still in my back pocket. Denver's fingers still tapping the kitchen table. I see me reaching across the table. One by one I cut them off with my knife.

DENVER: So. What's up? Jude?

JUDE: I have something I want to tell you.

DENVER: Yeah?

JUDE: It involves a dead body.

DENVER: What? You and Ivan had a fight?

JUDE: On the glacier. This young kid. Buried in the ice. I found him. I cut off his fingers. They were sticking out of the snow, decomposing from exposure. I thought … I thought it might spread so … I don't know. I cut them off and put them in this freezer bag. You wanna see it? I'll show you. Out on the glacier.

SCENE EIGHT

DENVER: (*to audience*) Someone pulls out a bag of fingers, what are you supposed to think? I mean, they were the real thing. A quick glance is all I got, but long enough to know, you know?

Black and scabby. Bone sticking through.

He puts them back in his pocket. Paranoid. Like I'm gonna steal them and run.

He's out the door.

Jesus. You know someone. You watch videos with them. You eat dinner with them. Suddenly they're ripping fingers off some dead kid.

Makes you question their stability. Makes you question your own.

I think about that movie with the kids who find that body by the river. *River's Edge*. They don't tell anyone. They go out and hang with it. Crispin Glover and Keanu Reeves. I remember being disturbed by that movie.

I finally catch up. Jude is crouched down beside a rock. He's got this look on his face, like a small child trying to figure out a puzzle.

I walk up behind him.

JUDE: There he is.

DENVER: Let's have a look, kiddo.

(*to audience*) Jesus, where did that sentence come from? I hear my father's voice.

This thing … this … corpse … is … it isn't …

Through the ice, in the dark, I see him.

His body, strips of leather, pieces of bark. His large face, sunken, hollow. His eyes empty. His mouth open. *Night of the Living Dead*. Like something you'd see in a museum.

I stand there stunned.

JUDE: You think I did the right thing? With the fingers? I mean – I don't know.

SCENE NINE

(Marjorie is eating a can of soup.)

DENVER: Are you listening to this? Marjorie? Are you listening?

MARJORIE: A body in the snow.

DENVER: I want you to listen.

MARJORIE: I'm listening.

DENVER: It's old. It's fucking … old. It's … like … I don't know … from another time … National Geographic territory … you know? 10,000 years maybe. Jesus, it's possible. I don't know.

Marjorie?

MARJORIE: (*to audience*) I don't really have anything to say. I mean, should I feel excited? Scared? Moved?

I don't know.

I don't.

I'm thinking, this canned soup tastes fantastic. A little salty, but still – I could easily have another one.

Denver goes on and on. The grotesque features, the historical implications, the fingers in Jude's pocket. On and on. 'We've got to watch out for him,' he says.

DENVER: He's gone a bit ... I don't know ... something about him. You remember Crispin Glover in *River's Edge*? Well, I'm just saying, we'd better keep an eye. In the meantime –

MARJORIE: (*to audience*) On and on.

DENVER: We've got to figure this out. We can't just leave it out there.

MARJORIE: (*to audience*) It's three in the morning. My shoulders ache. There's a fresh pile of kindling by the stove. Does he even notice?

DENVER: We have to contact someone. I mean ... But – who? Who do you phone? Is there some kind of department? Is it a police matter?

Marjorie?

Marjorie?

MARJORIE: (*to audience*) 10,000 years, he says. What is that? What does it mean? I try to imagine it. I try to see it. I say it to myself under my breath.

10,000 years. 10,000 years.

It's not real to me. It means nothing. This body. This dead kid. It means nothing.

Denver's still talking. His words fly through me. They don't touch me at all.

DENVER: The Internet. Mrs. Cran.

SCENE TEN

JUDE: (*to audience*) His arm starts to melt through the ice. His forearm, his elbow. I sit there and watch it. Hour after hour. The sun cracking the ice around it. His skin black and starting to bubble. Reaching up out of the ice. Reaching up to me.

I wipe the moisture off it. Try to be gentle and soothing.

His skin ... his muscle ... it falls apart when I touch it. His arm is cooking. I ice it. Keep it cool. Stop the blistering.

I sit there for hours. The sun making me dizzy. The cold making me sleepy. I drift in and out.

I see my mother. She's got a cold washcloth on my face. I'm feverish and shaky. She's over me being gentle.

'There, there,' she says. 'My little fella, out in the snow all day, icicles for fingers. Gonna turn into a snowman, you are. My baby's got a glacier for a sandbox. What are you looking for out there? What are you trying to dig up?'

My mother being gentle. My father being nothing.

My hands grey and swollen. My fingers numb.

'Gonna hafta cut them off,' Dad says. 'Get the axe, Ma.'

I look at him. His big hands.

'Put them under your pillow, the finger fairy'll come and reward you, a quarter a finger. You'll be a rich man, kiddo.'

Mom wraps my hand in a cloth. She sits there looking out the window. 'What are you looking for? Nothing lives out there, nothing lives in ice.'

The sun still burning ... my snowman ... his biceps ... his shoulder ... everything rotting.

SCENE ELEVEN

DENVER: (*to audience*) It's 8:30 a.m. and I'm on my way to the library. I'm anxious to get a move on this before Jude goes total wacko and starts chopping the dead kid to pieces. Collecting him in freezer bags. Hoarding him away like a stamp collection.

I run into those fucking Nintendo kids.

The bulldog rolling a cigarette.

'Hey, Mister Shithead, got any games? Hey, shithead.'

The Rasta boys waving their hands and fingers around like they're made of joysticks. Busting themselves up. Their white dreads dancing on their heads.

I just about slam them.

I don't.

'Next week,' I say. Bunch of fuckers. I'd like to bury them in the ice for a couple of centuries.

The library is empty. Mrs. Cran is a hospitable type but a nosy bitch at the same time. She logs me on and sets me up. An e-mail account. She stands behind me.

'You gotta pick a password,' she says. 'Something that'll stick with you.'

Nosy bitch comes to mind.

I'm in. Locations. Sites. Keywords.

Dead kid. Glacier. Help.

I locate a ministry. Then a department. Then a name.

Kim.

Kim. Assistant Head of Archaeology, Heritage Department, Alberta Government.

Kim.

I see a tall woman, dressed in leather, hair pulled back. I see her with a scalpel and rubber gloves. The ice kid on a slab. Her digging into him, having a look, giddy with excitement. Me behind her, fully erect, giving it to her.

'You find what you're looking for?'

Mrs. Cran is behind me.

Kim.

Kim. I found it.

Kim. Come and get it.

SCENE TWELVE

KIM: (*to audience*) Some guy in the Duke Tavern buys me a drink. A salmon fisherman.

We talk. And drink. He says, 'You're not so bad.'

In the Duke Tavern, that's as good as it gets.

I've been up here for two years.

If you said, 'Kim, you're going to end up in Edmonton making eyes at a salmon fisherman, I'd say fuck off.'

Not so bad. Not so good.

He passes the time. Between reports. Between bone analyses and soil samples.

The job posting came up. Assistant Head of Archaeology, Heritage Department, Alberta Government. A junior position, but still …

I thought, 'Hey, adventure!'

Ha.

A small cubicle in a 1970s low-rise. Lunch meetings at the Journey's End Motel. Road trips on crappy buses. Investigating every crackpot inquiry that comes in. Bored housewives thinking they've found the missing link. There's me, digging through cow fields and ditches, up to my elbows in old dog bones and moose carcasses.

Then. I get an e-mail. A fella named Denver.

Denver.

I think of an outlaw. A long rawhide coat. A chiselled face. A hard body.

Denver.

Says, 'Found a body Real old. National Geographic territory Come and get it.'

Come and get it.

Denver.

Mr. Yohundi, my boss, I tell him I got an e-mail. A body in the ice.

I lean over his desk. 'I got a hunch,' I say. 'Could be the real McCoy, might be worth a look.'

Mr. Yohundi looks up at me and winks. 'Off you go,' he says.

Off I go. Shower and pack. I smell like salmon.

A six-seater Cessna. Pilot named Brendan. Tells me a story of his son. Went down in a crash. No bodies found.

'He's out there,' he says. 'In the ice. You find him, you bring him home, lady archaeologist.'

He stares down at the glacier. His eyes tear up.

'That ice is full of bodies waiting to be found.'

He shuts his eyes and says a prayer.

I think, 'Keep your head, Brendan. Steady, unless you want to join your kid.'

'Bring him home,' he says. 'I wanna see him, say goodbye proper.'

Goodbye.

The plane lands. Where the hell am I?

Three teenagers are hanging on the curb snorting blow off a key. One of them looks up with a squinty eye and winks.

'Yo, pretty bitch, you want some of this?'

He rubs his hand over his shaved head.

I stand over him.

Denver. 'You know a fella named Denver?'

Denver.

SCENE THIRTEEN

MARJORIE: (*to audience*) A woman comes to my door with a briefcase. She's got a badge. An ID in her wallet.

Kim. A government archaeologist.

Here it is, I think. My fantasy. My excavation.

I stand there looking at her. Her small hands. I imagine her briefcase filled with delicate knives and scalpels. Small metal hooks and claws. I feel them poking into me, pulling at my skin. Me open on the kitchen table. Her hands inside me.

I start to feel excited.

She opens her mouth and looks around.

'I'm looking for Denver. Does a man named Denver live here?'

Denver. Yes. Denver.

SCENE FOURTEEN

KIM: (*to Marjorie*) I'm staying at the hotel with the blue porch. A bit drafty. Large rooms.

You could hold a jamboree in there.

MARJORIE: (*to audience*) A jamboree? What the hell is she talking about?

KIM: A woman at the desk, she told me it used to be a real hot spot, during the gold rush. A saloon downstairs. Gunfights and all. She pointed out an actual bullet hole just outside my door. That's a real piece of history you've got there.

MARJORIE: (*to audience*) Gunfights, she says. I'll get the shotguns.

KIM: I had a good breakfast at the café.

(*pause*)

A cup of cold coffee in the morning and I'm usually fine. But this morning I decided to go for the whole deal. Sausage and bacon.

(*pause*)

The whole deal.

MARJORIE: (*to audience*) Jesus. Get to the point. Why are you in my house?

KIM: (*to audience*) This woman, standing there like a corpse, looking at me but not looking at me. Creepy. Is this a game? Have I been lured out here by a crazy bitch? Have a thing for lady archaeologists? Gonna rip off my clothes and butcher me? Possible.

MARJORIE: You come to see that dead kid.

KIM: What – Yes.

MARJORIE: Poke around a bit.

KIM: Have you seen it?

MARJORIE: No.

KIM: The body ... A man named Denver sent me an e-mail.

MARJORIE: I live with him. He lives here.

KIM: I've come to investigate. See what you've got, aside from a bullet hole and a hearty breakfast. See if there's anything to it. To this ... dead kid.

MARJORIE: (*to audience*) And what about me? Investigate me, I wanna say. Forget the dead ice kid. He's nothing. It's me, Kim. I'm the secret. I'm the mystery. It's me. Open your mouth. Ask for help.

KIM: So. Denver. Is he here?

(pause)

MARJORIE: Do you want to watch a video? You can watch a video if you want. While you wait for Denver. We run a video store. I'll put one on.

I've got some things to do. Out back.

SCENE FIFTEEN

MARJORIE: (*to audience*) I put *The Clan of the Cave Bear* into the VCR.

'A strange woman invades a tribe of Neanderthals,' I say. 'Daryl Hannah's best work.'

I leave her there, in my house. I go out the back door and stand there.

I look around.

The trees and the ice. An old Ski-Doo. A pile of wood.

I double over. I start to choke.

I see him. The dead ice kid.

I see him come up blue and ugly out of the ground. Eyes frozen open, mouth cracked open. Looking at me with a smile.

'Marjorie,' he says.

He takes my hand. I start walking. North. The glacier stretching out endlessly. The sun blasting me. The ice melting every step I take.

SCENE SIXTEEN

DENVER: (*to Kim*) Who the hell are you?

KIM: Denver?

DENVER: Where's Marjorie?

KIM: I'm Kim.

DENVER: Kim.

KIM: 'Dead kid – real old – come and get it.'

DENVER: Come and get it.

KIM: Here I am.

DENVER: Kim. What are you –

KIM: *The Clan of the Cave Bear*. Daryl Hannah's best work.

DENVER: Debatable.

KIM: Marjorie ... your ... she had things to do. She put this on. She said to wait.

DENVER: We live together. She's –

KIM: She's a real crackerjack. *Clan of the Cave Bear*, I mean ...

DENVER: She's suspicious of strangers. Takes time to warm up.

KIM: A real sense of humour.

(pause)

DENVER: So. You came. You're here.

(pause)

KIM: I thought you'd be some kind of outlaw. Your name ... it made me think of a tall, rough man. Guns and horses.

(pause)

DENVER: You wanna see it? The ice kid?

SCENE SEVENTEEN

JUDE: (*to audience*) I'm standing in the doorway of the shed behind my house. My dad used to build things. Spice racks, a mailbox. One Christmas he made a pair of wooden reindeer for everyone in town to put on their lawn. They gave me nightmares. I don't like fake wooden animals.

I load up some tools and wood, some kind of saw, a hammer and a tin of nails. I put them on my toboggan. I drag them across the ice. To him.

'We need some protection,' I say. 'A roof and four walls. We need a home.'

Old pieces of wood stacked up. I nailed them together. I lay some boards overtop and leave a hole for a door.

I climb in. I lie on top of him and curl up around him. I take his hand and whisper in his ear.

'Home sweet home.'

I feel myself sinking.

SCENE EIGHTEEN

MARJORIE: (*to audience*) It's dark. The moon makes circles on the ice. I walk slow. A straight line in front of me.

All that flat space.

I get a chill. I feel eyes on me. I turn around. I see a wall of snowmen, surrounding me. Their cold breath on my face. Their icy hands pushing me forward.

I shut my eyes. Keep moving.

Then, in front of me.

A rotten hump sticking out of the white ice. A rickety little shack. I use the word *shack* lightly. Crappy wood piled up. Not much craftsmanship, not much skill. Like it was thrown together. But there it is.

An old toboggan upside down.

I crawl inside. Smells like rot and mould. Cracks of light coming in through holes in the wood.

I see two bodies sunk into the ice.

A black stump sticking out of the snow. Someone else curled up around it. Like some kind of bad corpse movie. A zombie person pulling the life out of someone. Pulling him down into an icy grave.

I reach around. Try to pull them apart. Stuck together.

Stiff messy hair. Messy hair.

I feel a lump in my stomach.

I get both hands on and pull. Skin on ice. A ripping sound. Then a face.

Big eyes. Wide open. Cold and sleepy. Nothing moving.

I sit there looking at his quiet frozen eyes.

They look like mine.

SCENE NINETEEN

KIM: (*to audience*) Denver throws me a snowsuit.

'Put this on. The wind picks up out there. It'll cut you in half. Suit up. I'll gas up the Ski-Doo. We'll go have a quick look at him at night. The glacier's a real trip.'

I stare at this black, puffy thing with yellow stripes in a pile in front of me. Covered in sawdust and grease.

When in Rome.

I stuff myself in.

I feel fucking ridiculous. Start sweating like mad.

What the hell am I doing? Standing in someone's living room in a snowsuit.

There's Denver. Long johns hanging off him. He gets a goofy smile.

'You really fill that thing out,' he says. 'Just one more thing.'

He goes to get some goggles.

I get this urge. A strong sexual desire.

Denver.

I'll bet Marjorie's frigid. Frozen solid, inside and out. I'll bet she hasn't gone down on him in years. I'll bet he's dying for some warm attention.

I wonder how people end up with each other. I wonder how people end up with no one.

For a moment I see me living here – making tea on the stove, watching videos on the TV, Denver outside fixing our Ski-Doo.

What is that?

You wander into someone's life. And you instantly want it.

SCENE TWENTY

MARJORIE: (*to Kim*) That's my snowsuit.

KIM: Marjorie –

MARJORIE: You're wearing my snowsuit.

KIM: Um ... Denver ... he said ...

MARJORIE: Why are you wearing my snowsuit?

KIM: We were going to have a look at the body. He went to get some goggles. He gave it to me. He told me to put it on, so ...

(*pause*)

I'm sorry. I didn't ...

MARJORIE: Denver bought that. One for me. One for him. Matching snowsuits. We walked around town in them. He thought it was a real laugh.

DENVER: Marjorie –

MARJORIE: She's wearing my snowsuit.

DENVER: I was just gonna take her out to see the ice kid. Show her around the glacier on the Ski-Doo.

Marjorie? You okay? Where were you? Marjorie?

MARJORIE: Jude's out back frozen solid. I found him lying on the glacier curled up with the dead kid.

DENVER: What?

MARJORIE: They were stuck together. I had to pry him loose. I dragged him back here on a toboggan. He's not breathing. I don't know.

You two look like a couple of real sweethearts.

PART TWO

SCENE ONE

DENVER: (*to audience*) It took a couple of hours to thaw Jude out completely.

We pried him off the toboggan.

Kim checked his pulse and his breathing like she knew what she was doing.

'We have to ease him back slowly, otherwise he'll go into hypothermic shock. Body heat,' she says. 'Get undressed, Denver.'

It's a good thing she was around. I would've just thrown him into a hot bath and hoped for the best.

Kim ripped Jude's clothes off and we brought him into the bedroom. She rubbed his body – his muscles – back and forth while I undressed.

Standing there naked. I felt self-conscious. There's my friend half dead and I'm thinking about the hair on my body and the size of my dick.

I climbed on top of Jude and wrapped my body around his. His skinny body brittle and icy. I covered him and breathed on his eyes.

For a while he didn't move. I thought we lost him.

He eventually came around.

Marjorie didn't lift a finger. She just sat there, on a chair, staring at the snowsuit.

'She's in shock,' I thought. Finding someone you like stuck to the ice, blue in the face. It must have shut her down.

I told Jude to stay the night. We'd keep an eye on him in case there was some kind of relapse. I didn't really know what I was talking about.

He didn't say much.

He looked small in our bed. I felt sorry for him.

Kim went back to the hotel.

I apologized for all the psycho behaviour.

Jesus, she musta thought we were a bunch of loonies. Jude freezing his balls off, shacking up with an old corpse. Marjorie being a zombie, going on about some old snowsuit.

We made arrangements to meet the next day.

I sat in a chair next to Marjorie and tried to make a joke out of the situation, to lighten things up. Everything was heavy.

MARJORIE: I hate those things.

DENVER: What?

MARJORIE: Those matching snowsuits. You said it'd be a laugh. You said it'd be cute. I thought they were creepy. Walking around in them, I felt stupid.

DENVER: What are you talking about?

MARJORIE: I don't want it. I don't want to see it. Get it out of here.

DENVER: Are you – What? What's the matter with you?

MARJORIE: I don't want it. Get it out. Get it out. I don't want it. I don't want to wear it.

DENVER: No one's asking you to wear the fucking snowsuit. Christ.

SCENE TWO

JUDE: (*to audience*) I could hear them talking. I was drifting in and out.

Denver on top of me. Rubbing me.

Another voice. A woman named Kim. Some kind of scientist. An archaeologist, I think.

I lay there.

They were whispering ... discussing things ... like my mental state. My unbalanced behaviour.

I hear words like *gay* and *alone* and *abandoned*.

He's talking like I'm some kinda pathetic case and she starts in being psychological. About attachment syndromes and phobias and seeing death.

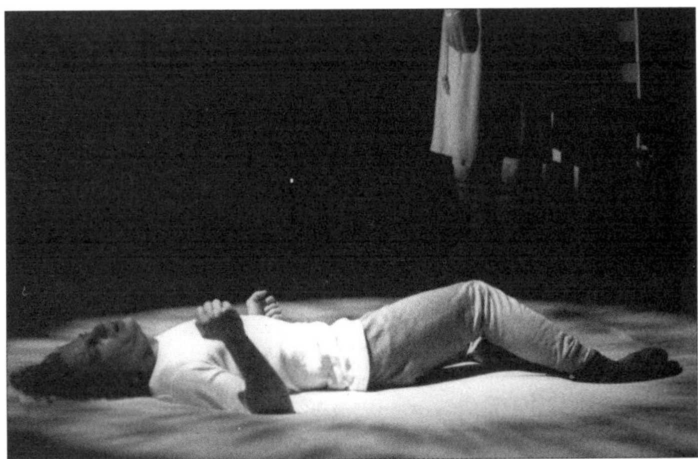

Jesus. No one knows me.

They start making plans. Excavation and removal. Dissection.

'The sooner the better,' says Denver. 'We'll go out tomorrow. You can pick around, confirm my suspicions,' he says.

She agrees. 'If there's something to it,' she says, 'I'll haul it outta there.'

I feel my small frozen heart start to thump.

'Bring it home with me. We've got facilities.'

The fuck you will.

My small heart jumping inside of me.

Denver's still on top of me. Me naked under the bedsheets. His cock on me. His hands on me. My body rumbles. Angry and sexual.

'He's coming around,' Denver says. 'He's coming back.'

He sends Kim out of the room.

'Don't want to shock him with an unfamiliar face.'

I open my eyes.

'Welcome back, kiddo.'

I smile.

'We'll take care of you.'

I lay there in their bed.

The fuck you will.

SCENE THREE

KIM: (*to audience*) I'm up all night, scratching like mad. My skin crawling. All red and rashed.

Mites … ticks … I don't know. I pick one out of my nose. What the hell – ?

That snowsuit. That fucking snowsuit.

Probably rolled up in a ball in a dirty shack. Infested. Now all over me.

I feel them inside me. Christ. Snowsuits and scabies. Frozen people. Read the signs, Kim. Pack your bags and get out.

But something … professional responsibility … curiosity. Denver standing there in his long johns with a goofy smile. I don't know.

I'm still here.

I do the whole thing. Wash the bedsheets. My clothes, I soak them in the sink. A hot shower. Scrub till I'm raw and blistered. Shave – my armpits, my pubic hair, everything.

I look at myself naked. Examine all my entries and exits.

I feel like a porn star. Shaved and wet.

I wonder if Denver's got a fetish for trimmed women.

He comes to pick me up. Nine a.m. sharp. I'm outside. My skin aching and rough. The wind cuts me.

He's on the Ski-Doo, all revved up.
I've got a scarf around my face.
'You ready to rumble?'
'Find me a drugstore, Denver. I'm infected.'

SCENE FOUR

DENVER: (*to audience*) I get her some kind of ointment.

'It'll send them bastard bugs screaming,' the druggist says.

We go inside. Kim's being icy to me. Understandable.

'I didn't know them snowsuits were bugged. I'll burn 'em,' I tell her.

She takes her clothes off. There she is, standing in her white underwear. Not embarrassed. But – raw.

The ointment in my hands. The sun in the window.

KIM: What are you putting on me?

DENVER: Comes highly recommended.

KIM: Read the instructions. I don't want to end up with a skin disease.

DENVER: You keep it on for an hour.

KIM: An hour.

DENVER: Then shower it off.

KIM: I don't believe this.

DENVER: Any longer it will burn the skin.

KIM: Burn – what?

DENVER: Just some ticks is all. We'll get them.

KIM: (*to audience*) Ticks, he says. He rubs the ointment into his hands. He hesitates. Come on, I think. Sterilize me.

DENVER: I packed us a lunch. I thought we'd picnic out on the glacier. Make a day of it. You can do your thing with the corpse. I'll build us a fire and heat up some stew.

KIM: (*to audience*) He walks towards me. He covers me in the ointment. Warm. Smells like him.

SCENE FIVE

MARJORIE: (*to audience*) I get up and make some soup. One for me. One for Jude. Something warm and comforting after his ordeal.

I tiptoe into the bedroom. The window's open. Jude's gone.

The slippery little –

Not his fault.

It's the dead kid. The dead kid's got a hold of him. And here I am. Eating soup in an empty house.

I sit on the empty bed.

I finish both cans of soup. It gurgles in my stomach. Something unsettled inside of me.

I walk into the kitchen. Look around.

I double over. Grab on to the sink to steady myself.

I feel him. The dead kid. Inside of me.

I open a drawer. Wash up a little paring knife.

Me over the sink.

I open my housecoat.

Shiver a bit from the draft at the window. Some caulking would be a good idea.

I make a little cut under my ribs.

A trickle of blood runs down my stomach and into my underwear.

'Get out of me.'

I say this in a whisper to the dead kid.

I feel relief start to come.

More cuts. More relief.

'Get out of me.'

Then. Someone pounding outside. I close my housecoat. I drop the knife in the sink.

Three teenagers in big toques crammed in the doorway. They start buzzing at me.

'Where's the games? Denver promised us some games. He said this week. Give it up, lady.'

I look at them. Their small faces twitchy and aggressive.

One of them, short, shaved, chews on his lips.

'We ain't leaving till we get our games,' he says.

Games.

All right then.

I invite them in. I sit them down on the couch. The three of them squished together. Their knees tight. Trying not to touch each other.

I'm quiet. They're still.

'You boys want to play some games, do you?'

One of them pulls his braids over his eyes. One of them looks at his sneakers. The short one says, 'Yeah.'

Blood starts dripping onto the floor from the cut on my stomach. A little trickle.

The boys look at it. They try not to look at it. I put my big toe into the blood. I make a little pattern on the floor. I look down into it.

Their awkward bodies frozen still.

'Unfortunately, I think your Nintendo's out of the question,' I say. 'I think Denver blew you off.'

I see them clench up.

'Perk up. All is not lost. There's something else better then video. A horror story rotting deep in the ice, infecting our pure white snow. A secret. And it's all yours.'

SCENE SIX

JUDE: (*to audience*) Sitting in my kitchen. Anxious and fidgety.

I walk around my house.

I go into my bedroom.

I pick some things up and put them back down. A book. A pillow. A sweater. A plate. Something familiar to calm me. To remind me.

Nothing comes.

I pick up a porn tape I stole from Denver and Marjorie. I look at the back cover and try to remember the movie.

I try to masturbate on the couch.

A little bit comes out. Not much. A trickle. More painful than anything.

Back in the kitchen. Standing in front of the refrigerator.

I take his fingers out of the freezer. Put them down on a tea towel and spread them out.

Cubes of black ice. I try washing them in the sink. Hot hot water.

They fall apart.

A few larger chunks ... pieces of bone ... get caught up in the drain. The water starts to back up.

I see him in pieces, lying at the bottom of the sink. Sediment, swirling around.

I put my hands in the water and gather him up.

In the water, I see her. The archaeologist. Her face. Her hands.

I feel her ripping into us.

Kim.

SCENE SEVEN

KIM: (*to audience*) Out on the glacier, everything blinding and white.

Denver's cooking up a storm. A real expert fire maker. A couple of twigs, a wooden match and *boom*! Flames shoot up off the ice.

That ointment seemed to do the trick. My skin's numb, but the itch is gone.

Let's get to it, I think. Let's unravel this little mystery.

I crawl into this old shack. I kneel down on the ice. There it is – a body submerged in the ice.

Jesus.

A child. Perfectly preserved – except for an arm, exposed and rotted. Missing fingers – an animal maybe – but the rest ...

I take out a flashlight and examine the corpse

A small oval skull, a high forehead. A twisted body. A small pelvis, thin legs.

Jesus.

I'm over the body with a digital camera. Examining the bones … the body … through the ice. Denver comes into the shack with a can of stew. My eyes light up.

DENVER: The lady archaeologist likes what she sees?

KIM: (*to audience*) That goofy grin on his face.

The can of hot stew falls all over the ice.

He opens my coat. His pants are off.

I'm on my back, rolling back and forth. Denver's pushing into me. I stretch and grab. Something frozen and dead.

Snap.

I rip the corpse's arm off at the elbow.

FUCK.

I toss it. It rolls out the door.

Denver's out of breath. I'm looking at the light coming in through the holes in the wood.

I see a shadow. A pair of eyes blinking. They lock onto mine.

They're gone.

Shadow tricks, I think.

We lie there together. Me, Denver and our dead, armless kid. In our little wooden shack at the edge of nowhere. A little family.

Denver pulls up his pants.

'Got to get back,' I say. 'Make some calls. We have to move fast. He's exposing at a fast rate. I have to get some people out here.'

We find our gloves stuck to the ice.

SCENE EIGHT

MARJORIE: (*to audience*) In the kitchen. I'm at the window. Denver's toolbox spread out on the floor. A caulking gun in my hands, filling in the cracks between the wood and the glass. Balanced on the sink, on my knees, reaching up.

The paring knife is still in the sink. Drops of blood on the floor.

I hear a tapping sound. Three faces in the window. The teenagers.

'Jeez, lady, you weren't kidding. That freak under the ice – we saw him.'

'And something else. Your man squealing like shit, someone on him, him on someone – that new lady, Kim – he and she melting the ice.'

The short one smiles. He looks around. He pulls something out of his coat. An arm. Black and rotten. He drops it in front of me.

'A souvenir,' he says.

I stare at the arm. Lying dead on my kitchen floor.

I look at the teenagers, shifting back and forth. Sweaty. Their awkward smiles. Their flushed cheeks.

'You have access to some shovels?' I say. 'Some sharp tools?'

SCENE NINE

DENVER: It's a real discovery, Marjorie. Could have important repercussions. To find a body like that, fully preserved.

KIM: It's too soon to make any conclusions, but –

DENVER: It's rare.

KIM: There's only so much I can do right now. But the features, the location. I won't know for sure till the forensics, the carbon dating, but it's enough, it's enough to warrant an investigation –

DENVER: She's calling them out. A whole team of experts. To have a close look.

KIM: Forensic anthropologists, glaciologists –

DENVER: They're gonna bring him up out of the ice. An excavation. Marjorie? Do you understand – ?

MARJORIE: You're shivering. Your clothes are wet. You've been playing in the snow.

(pause)

KIM: How's your friend? Jude? Is he – ?

MARJORIE: Jude?

KIM: Jude … isn't that his … ?

MARJORIE: Jude. Yes. I don't know. I woke up and he was gone.

KIM: *(to audience)* Marjorie's eyes locked onto mine. *Get the body and get out. Get out of here. It's not your mess.*

DENVER: What do you mean? Marjorie? Where is he? You were supposed to watch him. You were supposed to – Jesus, Marjorie. He could be walking around in shock. Marjorie?

MARJORIE: Oh, Denver. Some kids came by looking for you, asking about some kind of game. Nintendo, I think. Nice boys. Seemed a bit anxious.

DENVER: For Chrissake, Marjorie.

SCENE TEN

KIM: (*to audience*) I head back to the hotel. Denver walks me halfway, then veers off to look for Jude.

My mind's all over the place. I literally bump into a parked car.

Sexual and twitchy.

Denver inside of me. The large Mongoloid face in the ice. The eyes in the wood.

Those teenagers still on the curb outside my hotel. Perched there. They watch me walk by. Big smiles on their faces.

I think, 'Jesus, do something – play a game, go for a walk, you little vultures.'

The two Rasta boys practice a handshake. The short one licks his lips. Little creeps.

Say nothing.

Outside my hotel door there's an old bedsheet rolled up in a ball. Real quality maid service they've got here. I pick it up and place it on the bed.

The room smells antiseptic. The bed still stripped. My clothes still in the sink.

I get on the phone. I leave a message for Mr. Yohundi.

'Things checked out. Get a team together, charter a plane ASAP. The hotel with the blue porch.'

I take out my laptop. I e-mail him the photos.

Come and get it.

I crawl on top of the bed. Dizzy. Too much sun and ice.

I grab the bedsheet. Something inside, wrapped up.

It falls out. His arm. The corpse.

It bounces onto the mattress. Onto the floor.

SCENE ELEVEN

MARJORIE: (*to audience*) Denver comes home. He stands outside and kicks snow off his boots.

DENVER: I don't know where Jude is.

MARJORIE: (*to audience*) I look out at the ice.

DENVER: For fuck sakes. I've had enough of this.

MARJORIE: (*to audience*) He goes inside and slams the door. I stand outside in my housecoat. I lie down in the snow.

My whole body seizes up.

I vomit. A stream of liquid. Nothing solid.

Some of it on my chin. Some of it on my housecoat.

I get on my knees.

I throw up again. My stomach pulsing. Vomit all around me, seeping into the ice. It disappears.

I grab a handful of snow and bring it to my face. Into my mouth. More and more.

The clean and cold numbing me.

More and more.

I look out at the ice. Clean and smooth.

I look back at the house. Ugly wood and aluminum siding.

Denver's shadow in the bedroom window. He turns off the light.

SCENE TWELVE

DENVER: (*to audience*) In bed that night. Half asleep.

I hear Marjorie come inside.

The thought of talking to her – lying beside her – suddenly I can't bear it.

She makes her way to the bedroom.

I'm sweaty and anxious. Like I'm about to be locked in a room with a complete stranger with nothing to say. That heavy silence that makes you sick.

How did I do this?

For ten years.

How did we do this?

How did we share the same bed, every night? How did we get up, every morning, and be together? Seven days a week. Breakfasts. Conversations. What did we talk about? Grocery shopping. Watching videos. Touching each other. Having sex.

How did we do that?

I can't understand. It seems completely unbelievable to me.

Marjorie's in the bedroom, in front of the mirror. She opens her housecoat.

I have one eye open. Watching her.

She's got a bunch of little cuts ... slices ... on her stomach.

(*to Marjorie*) I burned those snowsuits. Kim caught something off them. Bugs. Musta been infested. I took them out back, put them in a barrel with some wood and torched them.

MARJORIE: I put some caulking around the window. The draft was getting to me.

DENVER: (*to audience*) Marjorie climbs into bed beside me. We lie there. Barely breathing. The house is cold.

SCENE THIRTEEN

KIM: (*to audience*) Sitting on the bare mattress. Fully clothed. The window wide open. The freezing air coming in, getting rid of the stench. The dead arm lying on the floor in front of me.

My mind races. Marjorie maybe? Those teenagers?

I feel a knot in my stomach.

I lie down and try to sleep.

I start to think about curses. Curses of the dead.

I start to think about consequences. Of awakening the dead.

Out of the corner of my eye. Something moving, shifting. The arm.

I hear a voice in the room.

Stop it. Go to sleep. But something –

I reach down and pick it up. Holding it in my hand. Looking at the broken skin. I trace my finger from one end to the other.

I feel it move. Something under the skin. Drawing me in.

I shut my eyes.

My mouth open. My breathing slow.

I start to feel heavy. I lie back on the stiff mattress.

The arm against my throat.

SCENE FOURTEEN

JUDE: (*to audience*) It's dark.

I make a couple of sandwiches at the kitchen table. Nothing much. Some cheese and tomatoes. Some margarine.

I sit there and eat them.

I finish off a bag of stale potato chips. A few oatmeal cookies in a tin. I finish them off, too.

A whole jar of ketchup in the fridge, perfectly good.

A little bit of coke left in some Saran Wrap. A couple of lines maybe.

I wrap the pieces of his fingers – what's left of them – in a tea towel.

I put the ketchup and the coke and the fingers into my knapsack. I brush my teeth. I walk around my house.

Everything quiet.

My bare feet against the wood. My face in the window. My parents in the driveway.

I go outside.

I load up my toboggan.

The wind slams the front door shut. The sound echoes and falls on top of the snow.

SCENE FIFTEEN

KIM: (*to audience*) Lying on the bed. The arm still on top of me.

Dizzy. Sweaty.

I try to get up.

I turn my head. Sitting on a chair, beside my bed. I see him. Messy hair. His face, young and beautiful. Looking at me.

He doesn't say anything.

He gets up and stands over me.

He wipes some sweat off my forehead.

He puts his hands on me. My body starts to convulse.

I feel him reach down into my throat. His small hands covered in blood. Going through me. He takes them out of my mouth. He opens his fists.

Nothing. Empty.

I open my mouth and try to breathe.

He turns and goes into the bathroom. He comes back with a towel. He takes the arm from me and wraps it up delicately.

He walks out the door.

I'm stuck to the mattress.

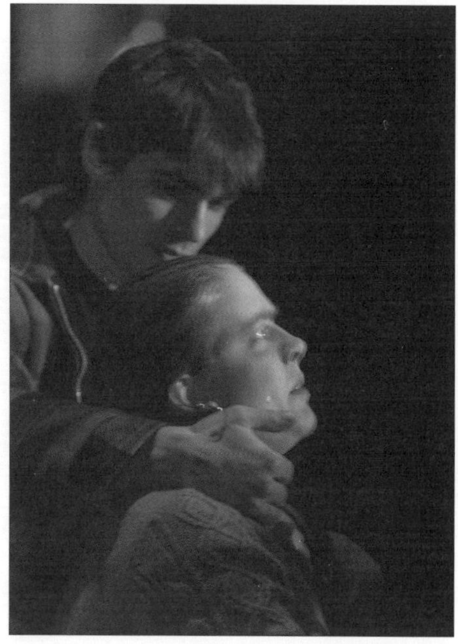

SCENE SIXTEEN

JUDE: (*to audience*) I head over to Denver and Marjorie's. Slip in the back door.

I put the ketchup and coke on their living room table.

I sit there for a moment.

I see the three of us. Me and Denver watching porn. Marjorie comes in with some popcorn.

We're sitting in front of the TV for hours. Night after night. Watching German men suck each other off.

Life can be strange and funny sometimes. I decide to finish off the coke. Three little lines.

I go into their bedroom. I watch them sleeping.

Denver's face all droopy. Marjorie stiff and tight. Me over top of them.

I sit on the edge of their bed. I trace the letters of my name with my finger on their bedsheet.

Jude.

I leave it there, between them.

I go out the back door. I don't make a sound when I leave.

(*pause*)

MARJORIE: Jude?

(*pause*)

JUDE: (*to audience*) On the glacier. In front of my shack. There's voices inside.

At the door, looking in, this is what I see: Three teenagers. One of them smoking, holding a flashlight. Two of them over my body, picking at it with shovels and some kind of garden hoe. A spade, I think it's called.

Chunks of ice all over the place. Some parkas in a pile in the corner. They're stripped down to their T-shirts. White dreadlocks stuck to their foreheads.

Soaked. Sweaty. Teenagers.

'Damn, this is fucking work,' they say. 'What the fuck we gonna do with this thing?'

The short one, still smoking, flicks ashes onto the ice.

'Stuff it. A lawn ornament, bitch.'

'Fuck it.'

They throw down their shovels.

The short one finishes his smoke, puts on a pair of work gloves and moves to my body.

'Pussies,' he says to the skinny white boys. 'I'll get it out, piece by piece if I gotta.'

He grabs one of the shovels. Aims it over my head. His muscles small and tight.

I dig my boots into the snow.

I pick up a chunk of ice. It starts to melt a bit in my bare hand. A little trickle of water slides down my wrist.

Some people's lives make sense. They follow some kind of path. They move forwards or backwards.

Some people's lives just stop.

SCENE SEVENTEEN

DENVER: (*to audience*) I get out of bed. My feet are practically numb and a sharp pain shoots through me when I step onto the cold floor.

I look at Marjorie stiff in her housecoat, lying on top of the sheets.

I think, that's it. When they haul that body out of the ice, pack it up and fly it out, I'm hitching a ride. I'm gone. Me, Kim and the ice kid, off to greener pastures.

There isn't a shred of regret in my head.

I sit in the kitchen and have some coffee. I'm not big on breakfast.

I wonder what time Kim's team is arriving. I sit there and listen for the sound of a plane.

I picture them like some kind of emergency crew. Flying in. A bunch of guys in orange medical gear with body bags, buzz saws and shit.

I don't know. It's just what came into my head.

I think of Jude. I think of him, clutching onto that freezer bag full of fingers. Marjorie sitting beside him, wearing a half-burnt snowsuit she dug out of the trash. Porn playing on the TV but no one's watching it.

God. What a strange, pathetic picture.

The loud buzz of a helicopter outside. It flies over the house and out onto the glacier. I can see it through the kitchen window.

I pull up on my Ski-Doo in front of Kim's hotel.

She's fully dressed, sitting on the edge of her bed. Her bags packed at her feet.

I tell her, 'Let's move. Your team is here. Helicoptered in about twenty minutes ago. They're already out on the glacier. Let's go.'

She looks at me with a strange, quiet look.

KIM: No. I'm not going anywhere. I'm staying here. I'm not going outside.

DENVER: (*to audience*) She starts going on about –

KIM: This place ... the corpse ...

DENVER: (*to audience*) ... some arm ... I don't know. She's not making sense. She doesn't look at me.

KIM: I'm staying here. I'm waiting for Mr. Yohundi. He can deal with this. Not me. I'm not going out there. I'm going home. Just – just leave me alone. Please.

DENVER: (*to audience*) What is this? Yesterday she's putting me inside her. Today she's shoving me out.

I notice the empty bottle of ointment on her dresser. Maybe some of those ticks got to her head.

I don't know.

KIM: Get out.

DENVER: (*to audience*) Fuck it. Every man for himself. I'm gone.

Out on the glacier. There's a helicopter parked next to the old shack. It's still running. People moving around. No one even stops to look at me.

Much to my surprise, it's pretty close to the scene I imagined.

I watch two men bring a body out of the shack.

SCENE EIGHTEEN

MARJORIE: (*to audience*) He says to me, 'Marjorie.' That's all he says. He sits on the end of the bed.

I'm still in my housecoat.

He's very soft. His cheeks are red and windburnt.

It looks like he wants something. Something intimate.

I have nothing to offer him. Anything I say ... anything I do ... it would seem false.

So I do nothing.

And he tells me.

(pause)

(Marjorie looks at Denver.)

(pause)

He tells me what he saw on the glacier this morning.

There was an ambulance helicopter hovering over the ice. Some paramedics running around with medical equipment and a stretcher.

A few RCMP officers huddled on the ice, talking to two teenagers, wrapped in orange blankets. Their long white dreadlocks tied back off their faces. Their eyes were red.

The Nintendo kids and their parents.

Looking distraught.

I don't think he used the word *distraught*. I think he said *blank*. Looking blank.

They rolled the stretcher out of the shack. The wheels got caught and slipped on the ice, and the whole thing almost collapsed.

There was someone on the stretcher, hooked up to an IV or something.

It was the other kid. The bulldog, Denver called him.

He was wearing some kind of head brace.

When they pulled him out, his two friends couldn't look at him.

They got him onto the helicopter and it took off. It was gone.

The RCMP were still digging around on the ice. Drinking coffee.

Denver got off his Ski-Doo and walked up to the shack. No one stopped him. Everyone was preoccupied.

DENVER: (*to audience*) I went inside. The air was stale. It smelled like rotten meat.

There were some parkas piled up in the corner. An empty can. Shovels. Chunks of ice. Splashes of blood against the wood walls of the shack. Some of it on the snow.

A large messy hole in the middle of the ice. I bent down and looked inside. There was nothing there.

Nothing.

It was gone. The ice kid.

Everything was gone.

MARJORIE: (*to audience*) One of the RCMP guys asked Denver what he was doing.

He said he was out for a ride on his Ski-Doo.

They told him to beat it. They were investigating a crime. A brutal assault. Some poor kid got whacked. A hole right through his skull.

The other two kids were lucky. They got away, the officer said.

Denver got back on his Ski-Doo.

He looked out at the ice.

DENVER: (*to audience*) I thought about Jude and his big eyes. I thought about him leading an army of snowmen across the glacier. Heading north.

That is an image that will come back to me often over the years.

SCENE NINETEEN

KIM: (*to audience*) Marjorie shows up at the hotel.

Mr. Yohundi and a few others were already in my room. We were just about to go downstairs and have one of those hearty breakfasts.

They said, 'You look like shit, Kim.' They said, 'A decent meal will fix you right up.'

Marjorie was very clear-headed. She spoke about Jude, and the teenagers, and the attack and the missing corpse.

She told us to forget the whole thing and go home.

Mr. Yohundi didn't seem phased at all.

He put his hands on my shoulders.

He whispered to me. 'Well, we've come all this way, might as well check out the breakfast.'

He left his card with the RCMP in case anything turned up.

It's amazing how easy it is for me to leave things behind. To bury them. To forget them.

I have this ability to move on. I'm not saying it's better or worse – I'm not saying it's a healthier way to live.

It's just that –

I don't know how people can get up every day if they don't. I don't know how people can make dinner and buy things and talk to people if the past is always swimming around in their brains.

I don't know. It would kill me.

I go back to Edmonton.

To the quiet torture of ugly office buildings, the Duke Tavern and the boardroom at the Journey's End Motel.

I guess at some point I'll hear a name, or see a face. And I'll be brought back here.

But tonight I'm doing my laundry and meeting up with some friends for drinks.

SCENE TWENTY

MARJORIE: Pick a direction and let's go.

(pause)

Denver?

(pause)

DENVER: *(to audience)* We decided to stick around.

I guess we could've left, but we couldn't figure out where to go. So we stayed put.

At first, Marjorie was implicated in the assault on the teenager. They thought she might have been some kind of accomplice.

I never thought of Marjorie as an accomplice type.

The kid recovered, except for a bad speech impediment and a complete short-term memory loss. The type of thing where you don't remember if you ate breakfast, but you can remember your first bike.

Marjorie was eventually cleared.

They blamed the attack on Jude. Thought maybe his past caught up to him and he went ... berzerk ... or something.

You know. Abandoned. A loner. Sexually confused. All that rage buried inside him. One day he just goes off.

I don't know. That's what they put in their report. I think there's still a warrant out for his arrest.

The Nintendo and PlayStations finally arrived. And the porn. It took about a month longer than they promised. Said they had trouble finding the place.

I don't know what happened.

GIRLS! GIRLS! GIRLS!

girls! girls! girls! was first produced by Teatro Comaneci at the Montreal Fringe Festival in June 2000.

This production was remounted as part of Montreal's Féstival de théâtre des Amériques (June 2001).

Puss: Alison Darcy
Jam: Julie Tamiko Manning
Splitz: Laura Teasdale
Little Bucky the Fag: Brendan Healy
Missy the Titless Bitch: Stephanie Buxton

Directed by Peter Hinton
Set and costume design by Eo Sharp
Lighting design by David Perreault Ninacs
Sound design by Troy Slocum
Stage management by Emma Tibaldo
Produced by Esme Terry and Teatro Comaneci

girls! girls! girls! was written, workshopped and developed with the generous assistance of the following: the Toronto Arts Council, the Canada Council for the Arts, Playwrights' Workshop Montreal, Buddies in Bad Times Theatre's 2000 Rhubarb! Festival and the Toronto Writers Cabal (John, Ian, Rebecca, Anton, Gill, Emily).

My sincere thanks to Peter Hinton and Teatro Comaneci.

CHARACTERS

PUSS
fourteen years old, a goth

JAM
fourteen years old, a goth

SPLITZ
fourteen years old, a gymnast

LITTLE BUCKY THE FAG
fourteen years old, a skater boy

MISSY THE TITLESS BITCH
fourteen years old, a gymnast

PRODUCTION NOTES

The events of the play take place over the course of one Friday night in a small town.

The music and pop-culture references in the script may be updated to reflect the present time and place of production.

The violence in the script should be portrayed as realistically as possible.

Although fictional in its narrative, this play was written in response to the events surrounding the brutal death of Reena Virk in Victoria, British Colombia, and by the Columbine massacre in Colorado, USA.

'You want help? I'll help you.'
– Dylan Klebold

SCENE ONE

(The sound of about 15,000 teenage girls screaming hysterically.

Puss and Jam are hanging out, listening to Walkmans – they are never without them. The screaming builds in intensity and cuts out suddenly.)

SCENE TWO

(Friday, after school.

Puss and Jam are hanging out in a park behind school. Splitz stands in front of them, wearing a green ribbon.)

PUSS: Why the melancholy puss, Splitz?

SPLITZ: I was robbed, girls. Swindled out of my shiny trophy.

PUSS: Say it ain't so.

JAM: Not our Splitz. Swindled?

SPLITZ: It's true, Jam. I stand here trophy-less.

JAM: No trophy for Splitz? That don't sit well with me.

SPLITZ: The vault proved to be my undoing.

PUSS: Explain.

SPLITZ: Having breezed through both the Kawartha District and the Kawartha Regional Gymnastic Competitions with red red red ribbons on the floor, the uneven bars and the vaulting apparatus, I was sure to be a threatening presence at the Central Ontario Secondary School Association finals in Peterborough.

I was eyeballed by the competition, girls. Ponytail whipped. It was nail-biting tense. But your Splitz was unshakable. I chalked up and pulled through with a stellar performance. The judges were kissing my tits, rewarding me with red red red all round. I was poised for the podium at the upcoming OFSSA finals, which you know transpired this past Wednesday-Thursday-Friday in the picturesque town of Brockville.

I was billeted at the welcoming home of Mr. and Mrs. Richard Westin, who graciously offered up their spare bedroom for my stay in the riverside community, along with a no-holds-barred seafood feast at the local Red Lobster, for which they footed the bill.

A tragic note, however, underlay the otherwise pleasing meal, as the Westins recounted the sad sad tale of their cancer-ridden daughter dying a hospital death just last year, thus freeing up the aforementioned bedroom, complete with a four-poster bed of which I took full advantage.

Did I mention the breadsticks? Damn fine sticks, girls.

PUSS: Take us to the climax of your undoing, Splitz.

SPLITZ: In that case, girls, we're standing in front of the vault. Yours truly was swimming through the competition, as per usge, with one run skip and a jump away from another red ribbon day.

I hit the horse with a steady leap. I tucked my tits tight. I spun like a well-told tale. I planted my feet on the mat –

JAM: Our Splitz poised for victory.

SPLITZ: And this, girls, is where it gets dirty.
Splitz had a tumble. Splitz went ass-backward. Knees buckled and tits up. Your Splitz. No red for Splitz. Just a 6.8. Just a fourth place. No climbing the podium for Splitz. Splitz wasn't to be climbing anywhere that day. It was the back of the bus for yours truly. It was a sad sad day in picturesque Brockville for Splitz. Trophy-less Splitz.

(Puss and Jam look at each other. They are floored.)

JAM: Shit, Splitz. That's a damn disappointment. That's a heartfelt loss.

PUSS: That's a fucking injustice. That's a kick to the head.

(Little Bucky the Fag enters, a bow and a quill of arrows fastened on his back.)

PUSS: It's Little Bucky the Fag.

JAM: Hey, Little Bucky.

LITTLE BUCKY: What's up? What's with the sour squeaks of your voices, gals?

JAM: It's about all we can muster. Splitz dropped a bombshell.

LITTLE BUCKY: What's the tragedy?

JAM: Splitz was just recounting her sad travails on the vaulting horse.

PUSS: Splitz went ass-backwards into a fourth-place finish at the OFSSA finals.

LITTLE BUCKY: Goddamn.

PUSS: Our Splitz, graceful and good, a sure thing, numero uno across the board three years running. Shoulda walked out on top. But one slippery trip-up and our champ is a chump. Life's a dirty slap in the face.

LITTLE BUCKY: Shit.

(Splitz collapses on the ground.)

PUSS: How's about a pick-me-up, Little Bucky? How's about showing us your wiggly-piggly?

JAM: Wiggly-pigglies cheer us up. And we need cheering up.

PUSS: We need Little Bucky to buck us up.

LITTLE BUCKY: I suppose a peek may be in order, Puss.

(Little Bucky drops his pants and wiggles his cock around. Puss and Jam squeal with delight.)

JAM: Sweet sweet sweet. That's a sight. Your sweet wiggly-piggly. Whaddya say, Splitz?

SPLITZ: A wiggly-piggly ain't gonna turn this green ribbon red.

PUSS: How's about a suck then? How's about a suck suck for Splitz on yer sweet lolly lolly, Little Bucky? How's about it?

LITTLE BUCKY: I suppose a suck suck could be in order, considering the dire day it's been for our Splitz. Whaddya say, Splitz?

(Splitz doesn't move.)

Well well well. It's a desperate day when Little Bucky can't buck up his gal pal Splitz.

(Little Bucky pulls up his pants and sits down. He blows a bubble. He pops it.)

SPLITZ: It's eating me up, girls.

JAM: What's that, Splitz?

PUSS: Tune in, Jam. Our Splitz got ripped.

SPLITZ: Ripped open and ripped off.

PUSS: It ain't right. Some titless bitch walking the streets basking in red while our Splitz sits here wallowing in green. It ain't right.

JAM: Ah, green's not so bad. Jam likes green. Green's a colour Jam can appreciate. Green's got a real beauty to it.

PUSS: Some glory-snatcher riding sky high while our Splitz is stuck in the dumps.

JAM: I could fuck green. I swear I could. Green makes me cum. Green's good.

SPLITZ: It's eating me up.

(pause)

LITTLE BUCKY: Little Bucky is thinking what we need is a di-ver-sion. That's what Little Bucky is thinking. Something to tame that sour taste of defeat. Maybe a little adventure is in order on this Friday eve. What say we take a stroll into the deep dark woods surrounding our humble community? What say we pull a Hansel and Gretel and get lost? What do you say? While our school chums are picking vomit out of their pigtails after a chug-a-lug from the parental units' private liquor stash, we'll be out cavorting with Mama Nature. Looking for a trail of breadcrumbs that'll lead us out of this misery, this standing around, 'cause life don't hafta be a fourth-place finish, gals. Life don't hafta be a green ribbon.

PUSS: I dunno, Little Bucky. I'm up for a booze-up myself. Jam?

JAM: Booze-up booze-up booze-up.

LITTLE BUCKY: I say it's up to Splitz. Let Splitz be the deciding factor. What's it gonna be, Splitz?

PUSS: What's it gonna be, chum?

(Splitz looks down at her green ribbon.)

SPLITZ: It's eating me up. Fucking eating me up.

(A blast of pop music.)

SCENE THREE

(A forest, later that night. Puss and Jam are listening to their Walkmans. Splitz is doing the splits, an apple balanced on her head. Little Bucky has an arrow aimed at her.)

LITTLE BUCKY: Little Bucky the archer, that's me. Number one with a bow. Little Bucky's got a big strong shaft and knows where to aim it, knows how to stick it. Never much for balls, soccer or otherwise. Never much for a toss and a throw in the football field. No, archery's my game. Hiding out in the woods with my merry merry band of teenage outlaws. Puss and Jam, Little Bucky and –

(Little Bucky pulls his arrow back, ready to fire. Splitz takes the apple off her head.)

What's up, Splitz?

SPLITZ: I just ain't got the concentration for this tonight.

LITTLE BUCKY: So there'll be no target practice? Is that what you're telling me? Then Little Bucky'll sheath his arrow. Little Bucky will put it away. No problemo. See, it's all Splitz tonight. Tonight what Splitz says goes. Ain't that right, gals?

PUSS: That's right, Little Bucky. It's all Splitz all night.

JAM: Hooray for Splitz! Hooray!

PUSS: See, if it was up to Puss we'd be having a booze-up. We'd be tanked if it was up to Puss. But it's not. It's Splitz.

JAM: Hooray!

PUSS: So what's it gonna be, pal?

(Splitz stares at the apple. She considers her options.)

SPLITZ: Splitz has her mind on something. That is, if her chums are up for it.

PUSS: Puss is always up for something. Or nothing, as the case may be. Puss is flexible. Ain't that right, Jam?

JAM: Hooray for Splitz! Hooray!

SPLITZ: Well, then, how's about a little scavenger hunt?

LITTLE BUCKY: Little Bucky likes to hunt.

SPLITZ: Then here it is, boys and girls. Tonight we'll be hunting red. Red red ribbons is what we're hunting for. See, out there roaming our streets is a wee titless beast. A slippery thing that's got something your darling Splitz oh so desires. And what you're gonna do, what you're gonna do, chums of mine, is locate this swindler and bring her back to yours truly.

PUSS: Puss likes the sound of this. Puss thinks this is better than a booze-up.

JAM: Booze-up booze-up booze-up.

SPLITZ: A red ribbon. That's what Splitz wants.

PUSS: And whatever Splitz wants …

SPLITZ: Go find that titless bitch with the red red ribbon and your Splitz will be a happy camper.

(Splitz takes a bite out of the apple. Puss and Jam dance. A blast of pop music.)

SCENE FOUR

(Puss and Jam are walking down Main Street armed with ski goggles and their Walkmans.)

PUSS: Watch your step, Jam. It's enemy territory tonight. Watch out. Main Street's a freakin war zone. Everyone's cranked and looking for a perk-up. Adios Monday and Tuesday, see ya later Wednesday and Thursday, it's Friday night and life's worth living again. Celebrate with a gurgle and a wank. Yep, it's all grass stains and grunts. Soft little yelps coming from the public parks. Little Carla's getting it from the college boys again. I'm tanked, come help youself, boys, I'll have four of you to go. The wiggly-pigglies are flying tonight, Jam. Watch you don't get one in the face.

JAM: Duck 'n' cover duck 'n' cover duck 'n' cover.

PUSS: Yep, Main Street's a bleeding arsehole. Main Street's a dirty bum. Running mad with small-town studs and prom queens. Kids with kids living off a bit here and a bit there. Payday's two weeks away and we're already stretched like a rubber band. Dipping into baby's birthday money for a pack of smokers. It's tomato soup and crackers. It's staying in and trying not to slit yourself. It's looking for a laugh when all you wanna do is cry. It's looking for a silver lining when everything's shit brown.

Kmart's not so bad if ya dress it up a bit and your man's still stocked in the looks department.

A pair of jeans, a T-shirt and Calvin Klein'd be fucking sending him down the runway. Remember when you'd kill your ma just to catch a peek at him in his jockeys. Now he's naked on the bed and you're scrubbing his underwear in the bathroom sink and all you can think about is a washer 'n' dryer.

Life's a bitch then you die. Life's a bitch then ya marry one.

But Friday comes and life's a party. Drink till ya puke. Puke up all the tears you been storing inside ya. Mix up your disappointment with a double rum 'n' coke and spew it all over the ground. Clean yourself out ready for next week's fill of letdowns.

Listen up, Jam. Ya can hear the kiddies screaming from their strollers: 'C'mon, Ma and Pa, guzzle it and let's go – I'm freezing my little arse off out here. Pack it up, call it a night, let's go home and be a family – mommy and daddy and baby make three.'

'Ah cram it up, kiddo, it's Friday night. Mommy and Daddy are on a bender. Give us a break, wee one, ya know we love ya but your ma's dance card is full. Hang tight and tomorrow it's a trip to McD's for you – dream of Filet-o-Fishes swimming down yer soft gullet. Your ma knows what's good for ya.

JAM: Duck 'n' cover duck 'n' cover duck 'n' cover.

PUSS: Yeah. It's a horror show. It's *Night of the Living Dead*. Freddy Krueger'd be shaking in his boots. And here we are trying to wade through it. Trying not to get sucked into this swamp. No, Puss and Jam will have none of it. Not tonight. There'll be no booze-up tonight 'cause Puss and Jam are on a mission. Puss and Jam got an agenda, that's what we got. We got our eyes on a prize. A prize that'll bring a smile to our dear Splitz. And somewhere 'cross town our Little Bucky's on the hunt as well. His arrow poised and perked. Ready to snag tonight's kill.

(Puss and Jam continue down Main Street.)

SCENE FIVE

(Little Bucky sitting on the ground, all bloody and snotty. He has just had the shit kicked out of him. His arrows are broken, scattered on the ground at his feet.)

LITTLE BUCKY: Motherfuckers. Oh, yer tough. I'd put my money on you anytime, boys. I bet you'd give Tyson a run. Natural Born Killers is your middle name.

You walk down the street like it's yours.

It's four of you and one of me. Little Bucky didn't stand a chance.

'You mind if we share your bench, Little Bucky? Would you mind that? We'd like to spend some quality time with ya. Squeeze over, will ya, we got a real affection for ya, don't we boys?'

Sitting there all snotty and silent. Waiting for the inevitable. And they're laughing like this is *Saturday Night Live*. Then. Pop.

(A blast of pop music.

Little Bucky doubles over. He spits up blood.)

'Jesus, I seen my little sis put up more of a fight. Let's haul it, boys, this one's done like dinner.'

(Little Bucky pulls a piece of glass out of his face.)

Real ingenious what you can do with a beer bottle. Real creative and original. I'll give ya an A++. My face is a work a art now.

They're long gone but I can still feel them. Their hands smell like cum. They got pretty eyes. Dangerous and gorgeous all at the same time.

What's going on here?

Everything's mixed up. I'm bleeding like a pig on the outside but inside I'm hearing a different story. Something in my tummy says this is good. Something in me wants it. Wants them to come back for round two. I feel my wiggly-piggly start to dance in my pants just thinking about it. Put it on videotape and I'd be glued to the set.

The four of them going at me.

I'm a mess. Can't tell what's hurt and what's affection. Can't tell what's love and what's not.

Buck yourself up, Little Bucky. Your gal pals are counting on you. Don't be a letdown. Don't be a sourpuss.

A red ribbon for your chums. That's the truth.

Wipe everything else out so there's nothing left 'cept that shiny red glow slow-burning inside ya.

Stop thinking 'cause thinking'll get you nowhere.

Thinking's a dead end.

(Little Bucky reaches down and finds one unbroken arrow. He clutches on to it.)

SCENE SIX

(Puss and Jam at the edge of a park. Puss is smoking. They are watching:

Missy the Titless Bitch wearing a red ribbon, dancing, with a bottle of booze.)

JAM: Hey, Puss. I spy with my little eye …

PUSS: My Jam's got eyes like a cat on speed.

JAM: I spy with my little eye …

PUSS: Out with it. What does Jam spy?

JAM: I spy with my little eye …

PUSS: Is it a game Jam wants? Then a game Jam gets.

JAM: Something that begins with red.

PUSS: Well, let's see. Is it a red wagon? Is that it?

(Jam shakes her head.)

PUSS: Is it a red balloon? Is that it?

(Jam shakes her head.)

PUSS: Is it a red ribbon? Is that it?

JAM: Yeah for Puss, yeah.

(A blast of pop music.
Missy takes a swig of booze.)

MISSY: Ha! I'm pissed. I'm wrecked. Living it up and loving it. It's three tits to the wind for me. I'm celebrating. Yeah! Yeah! Yeah!

(Music cuts out.)

JAM: I got her in my sights, Puss. A wee titless thing.

PUSS: And what is she doing, Jam? What's our little prize up to?

JAM: She's jumping up and down, Puss. She's guzzling back the booze. She's got herself a crowd and she's the main attraction. They're on their knees to her and she's spewing like a gusher. I sense a celebration is underway.

PUSS: We'll soon put a plug inta that party.

(A blast of pop music.)

MISSY: I'm queen. Queen of the red ribbon. I'm pissed! I'm double pissed! I'm primed and ready for it. I'm fourteen years old and a champion. Life is good. Life is a ball of fun for me. Life's a ride and I'm on top of the rolly coaster ready to take the plunge. I can see my life taking shape before my eyes. I can see a wall of red ribbons. Everywhere I look I see a cheering crowd. Yeah for Missy! Yeah!

(Music cuts out.)

JAM: Shall I grab a stick, Puss? A stick or a pipe – what's it gonna be? Is it gonna be Puss and Jam in the park with a pipe?

PUSS: Steady, Jam. This ain't gonna be no smash 'n' grab. No. This is a delicate operation. Puss and Jam have got to be crafty. A couple of slippery eels is what Puss and Jam have to be.

JAM: Your Jam is on the plan.

(A blast of pop music.)

MISSY: Fill me up, boys and girls, and I'll tell ya again about my high-flying escapades over the vaulting horse.

(Puss drops her smoke. She pulls up her socks. Missy dances.)

SCENE SEVEN

(Splitz alone in the forest, French braiding her hair.)

SPLITZ: Well, Splitz. Now that we got this moment of peace and quiet, while we're waiting for your chums to track down tonight's prize, why not indulge in some soul searching? Why not take stock of your life? Let's see where you're at. A real critical examination, if ya please. Well let's see. Fourteen years. Stack 'em up and what do ya got? What's it look like? Draw me a picture.

There's Mommy. At the sink. Washing, always washing.

A new sofa coming in tomorrow special order and that means new drapes and who's got time to repaint these days?

She's white-knuckled and crying in the dishwater. Like *Better Homes and Gardens* is gonna show up and gun her down if her colour schemes aren't all lined up.

And there's Daddy. Say hello, Daddy.

Hey, Pa, it's your daughter talking.

He's tight-lipped. He's locked. Nothing gets inta him. Nothing gets out. Wanna burn a hole in his chest. Wanna take a pair of scissors, open him up and see what's inside. Dig around his toilet water just to see if anything ever comes outta him.

Little sis is in her room. Smart as a whip. Eight years old and drawing pictures that'd frighten Charlie Manson. Words like KILL and FUCK and KILL THE FUCKER across her Garfield notepad. Tacking it up on the fridge with a clown magnet and no one blinks.

And where's me in this pretty picture? Here I am. I'm over here. Say hello to Splitz. Sitting lonesome-like in the woods.

But not for long. Soon my chums are gonna arrive and it's gonna be Christmas in July. It's gonna be Santa time.

A red red ribbon for me. I can see it. I'd slit my baby sis for it. And that's the sad truth.

Splitz has been a good girl. And now Splitz is gonna get what she deserves.

(Splitz continues to braid her hair.)

SCENE EIGHT

(Puss and Jam in the park with Missy. Missy is pissed to the gills. Jam holds her bottle of booze.)

MISSY: It's a party now. Say hello to my two new pals, world. Puss and Jam. Puss and Jam and Missy. Now there's three names go together better than Jennifer Love Hewitt. Yeah, we're gonna be lifelong pals. I can see it, girls. It's in the twinkly stars above. I can see us going through it all together. High school prom, then college days, then the job market, then how time flies. I can see us all grown up. We're sitting in a kitchen with our grandkiddies eating cookies. We're talking about old times. The three of us. Looking back having a laugh. Yeah, I love you already. Give Missy a kiss on the lips. Let's dance in a circle. Turn up the tunes. Blast 'em.

I fucking love this song.

(A blast of pop music.

Missy dances madly in a circle. Puss and Jam smile.

The music cuts out suddenly.

Missy falls on her face, dizzy and drunk. She throws up.)

MISSY: Uh oh. I'm down, girls. Missy took a tumble. Missy's down for the count. Got puke on her party dress. Uh oh.

(Missy looks down at her red ribbon, covered in puke.)

Uh oh. Uh oh.

(She starts to sob.)

PUSS: What's with the waterworks, Missy?

MISSY: Sorry, Mommy, your Missy's all messed up, red ribbon's a messy mess. Run me a bath, will ya? Clean me up, tuck me in, sleep tight, don't worry, 'cause your good girl's coming home. Shh shh.

PUSS: Home? No no no. Puss and Jam are just getting going. Ain't that right, Jam?

JAM: I'm revved up. I'm a motor car.

MISSY: Sorry sorry, I'm sorry Mommy, I'm sorry, Daddy, sorry sorry sorry, good girl's all messed up.

PUSS: Don't get maudlin, pal o' mine. The night is a baby. We got adventures planned.

MISSY: I got a red ribbon. I'm a champion, ain't I?

JAM: You're tops, Missy. You're Nadia fucking Comaneci.

MISSY: I'm a champion – see, Mommy, see my red ribbon. Mommy, maybe you wanna put that on the fridge, maybe you wanna make me a scrapbook.

PUSS: Enough with the Mommy and Daddy, babycakes. Tonight it's Puss and Jam. Tonight Puss and Jam are gonna be your tour guides. And we got a lead on a blowout. A little surprise soiree in the woods. It's party boys and party girls swinging from trees. It's dancing under a full moon. It's fun and games. And it's all for Missy. Everyone's waiting for Missy the champion to make a grand appearance.

MISSY: Missy wants to go home.

PUSS: What's that? Did you hear that, Jam? There was something ugly about that last sentence.

MISSY: Home is what Missy needs.

JAM: Say it's not the end of the line. Say it's not lights out. Say it's not that.

MISSY: Missy says it's time to go. Missy says the party's over.

JAM: That makes Jam sad. That makes Jam wanna cry.

MISSY: Missy's all messed up. Missy's party dress is a mess.

JAM: You don't wanna disappoint your new pals, do ya? You don't wanna leave Puss and Jam high and dry, do ya?

MISSY: No no no, Puss and Jam and Missy lifelong pals but …

PUSS: Then Puss thinks Missy should up and rise to the occasion. Puss thinks we should fuck off outta this puke park and hightail it to this backwoods brawl. What Missy needs is a little adventure. She doesn't need home. What's home? Home is empty. Home is lonely. Home is lying in bed trying to sleep when all you wanna do is dance.

MISSY: Missy likes to dance.

PUSS: Then get up and give Puss a kiss on the lips. Let's cut outta here.

(Missy tries to get up. She can barely move.)

MISSY: Um …

PUSS: No problemo. If vertical isn't working for ya then stick to the ground. A baby crawl is as good as anything. And we're in no hurry. What's it gonna be? Is Missy gonna crawl hands and knees then?

MISSY: Missy's gonna crawl. Missy's gonna crawl.

JAM: Then it's settled. Lead the way, champ.

PUSS: Puss has an idea. Puss thinks we should play a game. How 'bout Put a Hood on the Crawler? What do you think about that game, Jam?

JAM: Jam likes that game. That game's good.

(Puss puts her toque over Missy's head.)

MISSY: Missy can't see nothing but dark.

PUSS: *(whispering in Missy's ear)* Dark is better than having to look at the shit floating around here. It's wide-eyed Puss and Jam should be complaining. We're doing ya a favour, pal. Just wait till we get to the celebration in the woods. It'll be moonlight and stars. You'll be bug-eyed.

MISSY: Missy feels sick again.

JAM: Okay, champ. Have another slug. That'll settle you. Now it's off to the races.

(Jam gives Missy a slug of booze. Puss gives Missy a kiss. A blast of pop music.)

SCENE NINE

(Little Bucky is on the ground in his boxers, covered in lipstick, a bow in his hair, his face still encrusted from the last attack.)

LITTLE BUCKY: Little Bucky's all fixed up. Little Bucky's all dolled up. Little Bucky's looking like a million bucks.

Look at me. I'm Kurt Cobain back from the grave. Courtney Love'd be falling for me.

You girls are fucking magicians with lipstick.

'Ah, what's the matter, Little Bucky? Looks like you've been through the ringer. What do you think, girls, we can fix him up, can't we?'

They hold me down on the grass while Mary Kay pulls out her purse. I'm struggling, but apparently field hockey really pays off in the muscle department.

'You're a pretty thing, Little Bucky. You're a real sexpot. Don't you go stealing our boyfriends now, will ya?'

I say, 'Too late, girls, I already had 'em.'

You fucking prissy pricks. Little Bucky could show and tell you things. They take my pants off. Then it's 'Who wants to go for a ride? I'll bet Little Bucky's a real bronco. Line up, girls, let's have a go.'

And all of a sudden I'm a ride and they're lined up in front of me. One after the other. They're on me. My wiggly-piggly is dead in my shorts. And they're screaming with laughs.

So here I am. Pantless and alone. And the night's getting cold.

Where's Puss and Jam? Where's my pals? Have they fucked off? Puss and Jam? Splitz?

(He looks around.)

No red. No pals. No pants.

Bucky's in a jam. Whatcha gonna do? Find your chums. That's what. Chums is good. They're waiting for ya. Yeah. They're teary-eyed, worried and running in circles. Listen. Ya can hear them hollering.

'Where's our man Bucky? Where's our lifelong bud? Wiggly-pigglies cheer us up and we need cheering up – we need Little Bucky to buck us up.'

What's ya waiting for? Go on. Hoof it. Get outta this mess. Find your chums.

Go on. Go.

(He doesn't move.)

SCENE TEN

(Puss and Jam are standing at the edge of the forest.)

JAM: Puss and Jam are best pals, ain't that right?

PUSS: Thelma 'n' Louise got nothing on us, Jam.

JAM: We're friends to the end, ain't that right?

PUSS: At the end of the day Puss is open-armed to you.

JAM: If Jam was in a jam Puss'd be there to pull her out?

PUSS: Puss'd jump in with both feet. Puss is Jam's life preserver.

JAM: What we got together is true affection. Would you say that, Puss?

PUSS: I'd say that.

JAM: What we got together is real good. Would you say that, Puss?

PUSS: What's with this sticky talk, Jam? What's with this mushy chatter?

JAM: Say that, Puss. Just say that.

PUSS: What we got is good. What we got is true affection.

JAM: That's good. That's real good, Puss.

(Missy arrives, still hooded, crawling slowly in front of them.)

MISSY: Here comes Missy, here she comes. Make way for champion. We're getting close, pals. I can hear them calling my name, saying, 'Yeah for Missy, yeah for Missy.'

(Puss hoofs Missy in the stomach. Missy goes down. Jam looks at Puss.)

SCENE ELEVEN

(The sound of about 15,000 teenage girls screaming. Little Bucky is still sitting on the ground, frozen.)

SCENE TWELVE

(The forest. Missy is leaning against a tree passed out, puke-stained and dirty, the toque pulled up over her eyes, Puss, Jam and Splitz in front of her.)

PUSS: She's wrecked. She's out cold.

JAM: She's caved in all right. Had to drag her face-up by the feet the last stretch and a half. Ain't that right, Puss?

PUSS: That's right, Jam.

JAM: 'Missy the toboggan,' that's what I said. 'Hop on, Puss, I'll give ya a ride.' I gave ya a ride, didn't I, Puss?

PUSS: A bumpy ride, Jam. But a ride it was.

JAM: There she is, better or worse. Better or worse there she is.

PUSS: Puss and Jam come through. Puss and Jam come up with the goods.

JAM: Yeah for Puss and Jam. Puss and Jam did good.

PUSS: Feast your eyes on that red beauty, Splitz. Flapping ribbon-like in the night breeze. Fucking elegance. I can see your attraction to it. Yeah, it's pure joy. A flash of brilliant colour. And it's yours for the taking. Go on, Splitz. Help yourself.

(Splitz stares at Missy.)

What's the holdup? You want Puss and Jam to do the honours? Is that what you want? Well then, step up to the podium, champ. And watch us turn your shit-green life into a shimmering glimmering red.

JAM: Yeah for Splitz, yeah yeah yeah.

PUSS: Hold her down, Jam, while I strip the bitch of her glory. Don't want her bolting up in a panic.

SPLITZ: Hold up, chums. Where's the kicks in robbing a corpse? Where's the glee in screwing a sleepwalker? No, girls. Alive and kicking is more fun. I want her wide-eyed and awake. I want tears and sobs. I want her terror-struck. That's what Splitz wants.

PUSS: And whatever Splitz wants …

SPLITZ: Splitz wants it slow and painful.

PUSS: Then slow and painful it's gonna be.

(Puss approaches Missy.)

JAM: Jam is feeling incomplete. Jam is feeling minus one. Where's our Little Bucky? Where's our little man? Is he still on the hunt? Have we left him high and dry?

PUSS: Maybe our Little Bucky threw in the towel. Maybe he's home in beddy-bye by now.

JAM: It's not like Little Bucky to peter out of a party. He should be here.

PUSS: Little Bucky can take care of himself.

JAM: Jam is worried. Should we gear up and get him?

PUSS: Puss ain't going back in there. Puss wanna stay here. Puss wanna get messy with Missy.

JAM: Little Bucky could be face down in the gutter.

PUSS: Or home in bed. Covers up. Lights out.

JAM: Jam says something ain't right.

PUSS: Puss says let's get on with it.

JAM: Jam sees trouble.

PUSS: Puss sees red.

JAM: Little Bucky's our chum.

PUSS: Forget Little Bucky. Puss is ripe and itchy for action.

JAM: What do we do, Splitz? What do we do?

SPLITZ: We wait for Little Bucky to make an appearance. Then it's gonna be fun and games for everyone.

(The girls stare at Missy. Puss smiles and pulls up her socks. A blast of pop music.)

SCENE THIRTEEN

(Little Bucky still sitting on the ground with his arrow.)

LITTLE BUCKY: Try. Try to feel something. Feel something good. C'mon.

What's the matter with ya? Are ya dead? Are ya a corpse? Are ya a fucking corpse, Little Bucky?

Care. C'mon. I dare ya. I double dare ya. Think of good things. Think of pretty things. Make something up.

How 'bout your ma and pa? Care for them. Your loving family. Try it on for size. Go on.

Care about your chums. Care about yourself. Go on. Try. Think of future things.

I look ahead and it's more of the same. I look behind and there's nothing there. I look at me now and wanna cry.

A deer in the fucking headlights – that's you, Little Bucky.

A Mack truck barrelling at ya full steam ahead and all ya can do is sit here and pull a zombie.

Yeah. Ya know what's coming. Ya can feel it.

Tragedy's coming in on the morning bus. It's on it's way.

Something bad is happening. Your head is making plans.

(Little Bucky takes the bow out of his hair. He wipes the lipstick off his face.)

SCENE FOURTEEN

(The forest. Missy is holding her head. Blood is gushing from her forehead. The girls surround her. Puss has blood on her sneakers.)

MISSY: Missy's bleeding. Missy's spilling blood. What's going on?

(pause)

Pals ...? Puss ...? Jam ...?

(pause)

I'm blinded. Can't see nothing but red streaks.

(pause)

What's going on? Pals ...?

(pause)

Pals ...? Where are ya?

(pause)

It's me. It's Missy the champion. It's me. I'm hurt.

(pause)

Please please please.

(Splitz moves to Missy. She crouches down in front of her face.)

MISSY: Jam? Is that you? Puss?

SPLITZ: What's up, Messy? What's a matter?

MISSY: It's Missy. It's ...

SPLITZ: *(to Puss)* Missy. Does that name ring a bell with you, girls?

PUSS: Nothing familiar is ringing in my ears.

JAM: Qu'est ce que c'est Missy?

MISSY: It's me. Lifelong pals. It's me. There was a party. Boys and girls swinging from trees.

SPLITZ: You hear that? A party. Boys and girls. Now that does sound juicy. That does sound like something I could really sink my teeth into. You know anything about this, girls? You know anything about this aforementioned soiree?

PUSS: I'm drawing a blank.

JAM: Nada.

SPLITZ: If there's a party, spill it, Messy. Spell it out. Don't hold back.

MISSY: What's going on? Am I ... Are we playing a game? Are we ... ?

SPLITZ: A game. There's an idea. What kinda game you wanna play? What you got in mind?

MISSY: No no no. Don't wanna play, don't wanna. No game. I'm I'm ... please.

SPLITZ: What's it gonna be, Little Miss Messy? You're all over the map. First it's a party. Now it's a game. What's it gonna be?

MISSY: I'm ...

SPLITZ: A party or a game. What's messy girl want?

MISSY: My head is sinking. Everything's a haze. I'm trying ta piece it together. I'm trying ta ... I was a champion. I met some pals. We was going to a party in the woods.

SPLITZ: That's fucking riveting. That's a fucking nail-biter. I'll be lining up ta buy the film rights to that story. What do you think, girls?

PUSS: I'm already waiting for the sequel.

MISSY: I'm cracked open and confused. Where's the party? Where's the pals? Where's help?

SPLITZ: Help? Who needs help?

MISSY: I'm bleeding to death here. I'm, I'm …

SPLITZ: You hear that? She's bleeding to death there.

PUSS: Well then, we'd better plug her up. Get the girl some gauze. Who's got the gauze?

JAM: I got no gauze. I got some gum.

MISSY: No no, Missy going. Missy going somewhere. Missy going home. This ain't no fun anymore. This ain't nothing.

(Missy tries to crawl away. The girls stand and watch her. She doesn't get far. She collapses face first on the ground.)

SPLITZ: Now I'm no nurse. I'm no nurse but I'm thinking that banging yer gushing head 'gainst the ground probably ain't the healthiest road to take. That's what I'm thinking.

(Missy sits up.)

MISSY: Ain't no one gonna help me?

(Missy cries. Splitz moves to her, delicately wiping blood and dirt off her face, out of her eyes.)

SPLITZ: Okay, Messy. Let's have a look. Let's have a peek-a-boo. Oh pretty pretty pretty. You're a real beaut. Open gash and all.

MISSY: *(looking around)* Puss? Jam?

SPLITZ: Say hello, girls.

PUSS: Hi, Missy.

JAM: Hi, Missy.

MISSY: Hi, pals.

JAM: What's up?

MISSY: Um … Missy was scared. Missy thought her pals weren't pals no more. Missy thought …

SPLITZ: Couple of faithful dogs they are. Couple of steadfast friends. Yup, they're true blue.

MISSY: … thought Puss and Jam left Missy in the lurch. But there ya are. Woncha come sit beside me?

SPLITZ: What about me? I'm right here. Ain't ya gonna say hi to me messy?

MISSY: It's Missy. I don't know …

SPLITZ: You don't know …

MISSY: … you …

SPLITZ: It's me. It's Splitz.

MISSY: Splitz …?

SPLITZ: It's Splitz.

MISSY: I don't know …

SPLITZ: Ya hear that, girls? She don't know. Now how'd ya think that makes Splitz feel? Left out and lonely, that's how.

MISSY: Missy don't mean to be mean. But Missy can't identify you.

SPLITZ: Course not. Missy's a champion. Missy's a high-flier. And what am I? What am I, girls?

JAM: What are ya, Splitz?

SPLITZ: I'm a letdown, that's what I am. I'm on the sidelines while you're on top. I'm down there with Mrs. Fifth and Mrs. Sixth and Mrs. Seventh. We're choking on bones while you're gorging on steak.

MISSY: Missy don't understand.

SPLITZ: Missy's tune is getting tired.

MISSY: What does you want?

SPLITZ: WHAT DOES I WANT?

(pause)

Well, let's see. Splitz wants world harmony and peaceful relations. Splitz wants hungry babies ta have their fill of sugary breakfast cereals. Splitz wants a balanced economic infrastructure.

But failing that, Splitz'll make do with your red ribbon.

(A long silence.

Missy stares up at Splitz. She starts to giggle.)

MISSY: Missy's having a sudden recollection. Missy's having a vision. Words like OFSSA and *Brockville* are flashing in my brain. Yeah. Missy's knowing you now. Missy's seeing you all geared up in front of the vaulting horse. Missy's seeing you in the air. Now Missy's seeing you flat out on yer bum. Missy's hearing gasps. Now Missy's hearing laughs.

Poor Splitz. What a tumble. What a riot. Give that girl a red nose and a squeaky toy.

And that opens the door for Missy. And Missy walks right through it. Missy don't choke. Missy comes out with the red.

There's cheers for Missy. And there's tears for Splitz.

Splitz is bawling baby-like.

It's BOO HOO in the locker room. It's BOO HOO in the showers. It's BOO HOO in the parking lot.

Meanwhile it's a celebration for me. I'm busting. I'm choking back tears of joy. I'm a champion.

Now Splitz wants to be champ. But she can't be champ. 'Cause Missy's champ.

Poor Splitz. Yeah. Missy knows ya. Missy sees ya. Missy feels for ya.

Poor Splitz. Splitz wants Missy's red ribbon.

But Missy says hands off. Missy says what's mine is mine.

(pause)

PUSS: You hear that? Little Miss Gash-on-the-Head says she's not gonna give it up.

JAM: Boo boo boo for Missy, boo.

PUSS: That's downright rude and unneighbourly, neighbour.

MISSY: Missy's a champion.

PUSS: Missy's a champion in the selfish-as-a-pig department.

MISSY: Missy's gonna stay a champion.

PUSS: What do ya think about that, girls?

JAM: Boo boo for Missy, boo.

MISSY: Missy don't like this party. Time for Missy to go.

(No one moves.)

Missy's going.

(No one moves.)

Missy's gone.

(Missy starts to crawl away slowly. The girls stand and watch.)

PUSS: Little Missy's taking off. She's taking her red ribbon and cutting out. How do you like that, Splitz?

SPLITZ: Don't like that. Don't like that one bit.

PUSS: What should we do? Should we just let her bail? After all the trouble we go to?

JAM: NO NO NO.

PUSS: Hm. It's a real puzzlement. A real tough equation. What should we do?

JAM: Don't go, Missy, don't go.

PUSS: Hey, Messy. We been talking it over and we're thinking you should stick around. We're thinking we should re-open this red ribbon debate. We're thinking you might come round to our way of thinking.

MISSY: *(still crawling)* Sorry Mommy, sorry Daddy. I'm coming home now. Your champ, your champ is coming home, red ribbon and all.

PUSS: Hey. Messy. Yoo hoo.

MISSY: Put me in a scrapbook, put me on the fridge. I'm a good good girl.

PUSS: Hey. Messy.

MISSY: I gotta go. Mommy, Daddy. Sorry. Sorry. I gotta go. Go home. Cause I'm champ champ champion.

(Missy stops. She vomits. Splitz loses it.)

SPLITZ: You fucking piece of misery.

(A blast of pop music.

Splitz rushes Missy and kicks her violently, repeatedly, in the face. Missy's head snaps back. She spits up blood. Puss joins in. Jam stands frozen and watches them go at her.)

SCENE FIFTEEN

(Little Bucky in a tree overlooking a park. He holds his arrow in his hand.)

LITTLE BUCKY: Streets are empty and quiet. But the park is throbbing soft and low. It's beer bottles and sleeping bags now. It's a quick wet fuck under the trees before home to bed. Everyone paired up and happy. Another Friday night come and gone.

'Ya love me?' she says. 'Sure do,' he says.

'Them faraway stars make me cry,' she says. 'Where's my fucking Calvins?' he says.

Oh, I'm tearing up. Yeah, it's real true love from where I'm at. Little Bucky's got a bird's-eye view of this X-rated mess. What a fucking perspective.

If ya don't like what you're looking at, stand on your head, see life a different way.

Yeah, now there's a prime piece of advice to live by. Real useful if fucking yoga instruction is yer goal. Right up there with 'Ya can be whatever ya want to be.'

I wanna be ... I wanna be ... I wanna be ...

(He clutches his arrow.)

I wanna ...

Get a girl in the chest. Get a boy in the head.

Little Bucky the archer, that's me. Number One with a bow.

Get a boy in the stomach. Get a boy in the leg.

Now they're on the run. Now the game's getting good. My wiggly-piggly's stiff and dripping wet. Line up, girls, Little Bucky'll take ya for a ride now.

Get a girl in the face. Get a girl in the back. Get a boy in the back. Get a girl in the heart.

What's a matter? Are them tears rolling down yer pretty cheekbones? Are them shit stains on yer fancy Calvins? Is that blood dripping down inta yer sneakers? Yeah, yer tough, boys, yer cracking me up.

(He looks down at his arrow.)

One lonely stick. It's all I got left. Itchy in my hands. I can feel ya quivering.

'Set me free, Pops,' ya say.

Okay, lonely stick. Friend of mine. Yer time's coming up.

SCENE SIXTEEN

(Missy leaning against a tree, truly fucked up. The toque is wrapped around her head, bandage-like. Splitz and Puss are sitting on the ground wiping blood off their sneakers. Jam walks over to Missy.)

JAM: Hey. Wanna listen to my Sony Walkman?

MISSY: *(she can barely speak)* Wanna go home.

JAM: Wanna get plugged in?

MISSY: Wanna go home.

JAM: Jam'll plug ya in if ya want.

MISSY: Wanna go home.

JAM: Don't be so fucking disagreeable, pal. Jam is doing ya a favour. It'll perk you right up.

(Jam puts her headphones on Missy and blasts the music. Silence. Jam looks around nervously.)

JAM: Stone-cold silence. It creeps round me. Everywhere I go it's there. Open a door. Set the table. Have a shower. Like some kinda disease. Some kinda cancer. I can see it spreading around. It's walking down my street and inviting itself in for Sunday dinners. Its fucking ugly tentacles reaching up and choking the neighbours. Pretty soon everyone's clammed up 'cause life is too horrible to say. All that's left is garbage talk. Make me puke. I'm throwing up night and day. And I'm dying to hear something real. Something. Shake me outta this stupor. Say words like *love* or *hate* like ya mean it and it's a fucking tornado warning. Say 'Life is fucked' and everyone's inside, windows shut, kids off the street.

Yeah, sentences are fucking deadly weapons in my house. Say 'Ma, I got a pain in my heart' or 'I'm so damn lonely' or 'I wanna kill myself' and everyone's sent into shock therapy.

Say 'Something's fucked up in this world' and Mister Silence sneaks up and slaps ya shut.

I got bruises all over me.

So I clam up.

Outside I'm stone cold but inside I'm raving. My head's busting.

'Gotta be numb, gotta be numb' – that's what Puss says and Puss is my chum. So it's Mister Sony Walkman for me. Turn it up. Volume 102. Till yer bleeding at the ears. Till blood and bones and questions and quiet are pouring outta you and there's nothing left inside but fucking sweet melodies pop popping away in yer head.

I look at my pals and they're a hundred miles away.

(Jam looks down at Missy.)

I look at her and see me.

(Puss looks over at Jam.)

PUSS: What's up, pal? What's with the tête-à-tête?

JAM: Puss ...

PUSS: What's with the private party over yonder?

JAM: She's slipping inta comatose land, Puss.

PUSS: Oh, I didn't realize you was the fucking Red Cross.

JAM: Jam is thinking this ain't too good.

PUSS: Didn't realize you was the president of the fucking bleeding-hearts club.

JAM: She's baked. I was just trying ...

PUSS: You was trying ...

JAM: ... ta perk her up.

PUSS: ... ta perk her up.

JAM: She's a bloody mess, Puss.

PUSS: Say it ain't so.

JAM: It's so.

PUSS: So?

JAM: So?

PUSS: So get those fucking things offa her scabby ears and come join yer pals.

(Jam doesn't move.)

Jam wants ta dance with the trash tart? Is that it? Jam wants to leave her pal Puss on the sidelines and go busting with Messy Missy? Is that what I'm ta take from this sudden turn of events?

JAM: No no no, Puss and Jam are lifelong but –

PUSS: Jam wants ta pull out on her chums?

JAM: No no.

PUSS: Then unplug the fucking bitch. Unplug her or I'll plug you, pal.

JAM: Look at her, Puss. She's ripped open and all sorts a ugly shit is pouring outta her all over us. Look at her. Look at us.

PUSS: 'Scuse me but I'm too busy looking at our chum Splitz. Remember our chum Splitz? Remember her in the dumps aching for a red ribbon? Remember us wading hip-deep through shit ta locate it? Remember us being lifelong pals? Is any a this ringing bells with ya?

JAM: I'm saying ...

PUSS: You're saying let's bail. You're saying let's be sweet 'n' sappy cunts. You're saying let's bandage her up and ship her back to Mommy and Daddy all safe and sound, red ribbon and all. Is that what you're saying?

JAM: I'm saying enough is enough.

PUSS: I'm saying unplug the messy bitch.

JAM: I'm saying it's too much.

PUSS: I'm saying come join yer pals and wait for Little Bucky to make an appearance.

JAM: I'm saying Little Bucky's a no-show.

PUSS: I'm saying Little Bucky don't bail on pals, PAL.

JAM: I'm saying what's done is done.

(pause)

PUSS: Are you hearing this, Splitz? Is this ringing shit-like in yer ears like it's ringing in mine?

SPLITZ: *(calmly)* Something's ringing in my ears, Puss. But it ain't the doubtful voice of our pal Jam. It's a sweet soft voice calling out ta me. A red ribbon voice whispering ta me. Beckoning ta me. Fingering me forward. Its sexy strains reaching 'cross the black night and grabbing my throat. Listen close, chums. Ya can hear it. It's saying, 'Come and get me, Splitz. Be a champ, champ. A red ribbon and all's okay. Little Bucky's a no-show? A no-go? No worries. Jam is squeamish and gutless? No problemo. I'm steadfast. I'm right here. At the end of the day when everyone's fucked up and fucked off, here I am.'

(Splitz slowly approaches Missy.)

Reach down inta your shit life and grab a hold a me. When there's nothing left ta grab, take what's yours. Fuck the consequences or the consequences will fuck you.

A red ribbon.
See it.
There's nothing else.

(Splitz stands over Missy, ready to pluck the ribbon off her chest. Little Bucky enters, casually clutching his arrow, still pantless, dirty and bloody.)

LITTLE BUCKY: What's up, gals?

(A blast of pop music.
The girls turn around.)

PUSS: Little Bucky!

JAM: Little Bucky!

PUSS: Well well well!

JAM: Splitz! It's Little Bucky!

SPLITZ: Just in time.

JAM: Little Bucky!

PUSS: Three cheers. The gang's all fucking here.

JAM: See, we thought …

PUSS: Little Bucky!

(Pause. The girls take in his appearance.)

JAM: You're cut up, Bucky. You're banged up. You're hurt.

(pause)

You're bloody, bruised and pantless.

(pause)

Little Bucky?

(pause)

Bucky?

(pause)

Don't just stand there zombie-like. Come and tell your concerned chums what happened. We was waiting for you. We was on pins and needles. Where was you?

LITTLE BUCKY: *(calmly)* Where was I?
Well, let's see.
I was lying poolside with Brad Pitt sucking back Coronas, chums. I was navigating the stars with Buck Rogers, chums. I was having tea with the Queen a Sheba, chums.
Where was I?
I was looking for your fucking red ribbon, chums.

PUSS: Take a gander, Bucky. There it is. In all its red glory. There it is. A diamond in the rough. Waiting ta be plucked.

SPLITZ: Puss and Jam come up with the goods.

LITTLE BUCKY: Well, congrats to you. I'm jumping up and down with glee.

PUSS: We been achy and itchy ta pluck it. But Splitz says hold off. Splitz says we wait for our Little Bucky. That's what Splitz says. Ain't that right, Splitz?

SPLITZ: That's what I says. I says tonight we all get a taste of red. Tonight we all get a piece.

JAM: See, we thought you was a no-show. We thought …

PUSS: But here ya are.

SPLITZ: Here you are.

PUSS: Feast yer eyes, Little Bucky. It's good. It'll cheer you right up.

(Little Bucky doesn't move.)

Go on. Have a peek close up. Maybe ya wanna touch it. He can touch it, can't he, Splitz?

SPLITZ: Little Bucky can touch it. Little Bucky can grab a handful if he pleases. If that's what Little Bucky wants. Splitz is no hog.

PUSS: Go on, Little Bucky. It don't bite.

(Little Bucky stares at Missy. He doesn't move.)

SPLITZ: Well then, Splitz will do the honours. Splitz will do it. Watch Splitz. Watch Splitz separate that red beauty from that scabby bitch. A messy business. But worth the effort. Ta be podium bound. I can hear the crowds. They're on their feet.

Yeah for Splitz, yeah for her chums.
There's Mom and Dad. Being proud parents.
Good for you, kiddo.
Good for me. Yeah. Fuck you.

(Splitz goes to grab the ribbon.)

LITTLE BUCKY: No.

(Splitz stops. No one moves.)

PUSS: What's that?

LITTLE BUCKY: I say no.

PUSS: You say no?

LITTLE BUCKY: I say no red.

PUSS: You say no red.

LITTLE BUCKY: I say fuck red. Chums.

(Pause. No one moves.)

PUSS: Now that's just harsh and hurtful, Little Bucky. That's just rude. After all we done. After us hauling that carcass 'cross town while you been playing hide 'n' seek. After us standing around picking our noses. Waiting for you. So you could have a taste of red with your chums.

LITTLE BUCKY: Forget red. Red's dead.

JAM: No no, red's not dead. No no.

LITTLE BUCKY: See, Splitz got it all wrong.

PUSS: Don't piss on our parade, Bucky.

LITTLE BUCKY: Splitz has been leading you astray, gals.

PUSS: Don't gum up our fun.

LITTLE BUCKY: We ain't champs, chumps. Champs is something we ain't never gonna be. Cheering crowds is something we ain't never gonna see. See, we're bottom barrel. We're laughing stocks. We're sad pathetic bumholes.

JAM: No no no.

LITTLE BUCKY: When moms and dads are tucking in their boys and girls at night, you know what they're saying? They're saying, 'Please God, don't let them turn out like them four unfortunates.'

PUSS: Clam it up, Bucky.

LITTLE BUCKY: And I say good. I say dance with that fact of life. I say pick it up and give it a hug and a kiss.

JAM: I got a kiss. Who wants a kiss? Kisses all round.

PUSS: Splitz. Strip the messy bitch. Go on. Have a taste.

LITTLE BUCKY: I got a new game and it's called Be the Worst Ya Can Be. Aim lower than low. Take what hope and ambition ya got left and burn them. Throw them off a fucking cliff. And watch life open up. Watch life be a party.

JAM: Kiss kiss kiss.

LITTLE BUCKY: Stop looking for red and say adios ta feeling blue.

PUSS: Splitz –

LITTLE BUCKY: Life's a cartoon. It's a dirty joke. So laugh it up.

JAM: This ain't funny, Bucky. This ain't good.

PUSS: Splitz –

LITTLE BUCKY: This game's over and out. Little Bucky ain't playing no more.

(Missy suddenly staggers to her feet. She wanders towards Little Bucky in a daze.)

MISSY: Pal? Pal? You gonna help Missy? I'm so full of pain. I'm so so so sorry. Good girl's gone bad bad bad bad. Mommy says life's a rosy place ta be, says life's full a pretty stuff, good stuff. Mommy, Daddy, where is ya? Where's the cheers? Where's good and pretty? I'm trying ta see but I need help I need help. You gonna help me, pal? Please please please, you gonna help Missy? Help Missy see pretty and good? Pal?

LITTLE BUCKY: *(softly)* You want help? I'll help you.

(Missy is standing, clutching on to Little Bucky. Little Bucky takes his arrow. He thrusts it through the red ribbon and into her heart.

A blast of fucked-up pop music.

Little Bucky continues to plunge the arrow through her. She staggers, falls to the ground, tries to crawl away, dies.

Silence. No one moves.)

JAM: Ah no. No no no. Poor red. Red's dead. Ah no.
Splitz? Puss?
Red's dead. Ah no no no no no.
What do we do?

(A long silence.)

PUSS: Plug in, Jam.

JAM: Puss . . . ?

PUSS: Time ta fuck off.

JAM: Puss . . . ?

PUSS: This party's kaput.

JAM: Puss . . . ?

PUSS: Plug in, pal.

(Jam doesn't move. Puss stares at her.)

Well.

(Puss puts her headphones on.)

I'm outta here, chums. See ya.

(Puss bolts.
Jam stares at dead Missy, unable to move.
Splitz stares at Little Bucky.)

SPLITZ: A piece of red. Shimmering and glimmering. A slice of beauty when ugly's everywhere. A dance when everything's standing still.

Splitz just wanted a taste. That's all.
That ain't so bad, Little Bucky.
We ain't so bad.

(Splitz wanders off in a daze.
Little Bucky sits beside Missy. He takes her hand.)

ABOUT THE AUTHOR

Greg MacArthur is a writer and a performer. His plays have been produced across Canada. Some of his writing credits include *Get Away, Snowman, girls! girls! girls!, Epiphany, The Rise and Fall of Peter Gaveston* and *Beggar Boy* (a play for children). He is the co-founder and co-artistic director of House of Slacks, a collaborative theatre company, whose work includes *The Millennium Project* and *Stem*. He has been Writer-In-Residence at the Writer's Network/Centre for the Book (Cape Town, South Africa); Playwright-in-Residence at Buddies in Bad Times Theatre (Toronto) and Artist-in-Residence at Playwrights' Workshop Montreal. His new play, *Recovery*, will premiere at the National Arts Centre in the spring of 2006.

Typeset in Sabon Next and Copperplate
Printed and bound at the Coach House on bpNichol Lane, 2005

Edited and designed by Alana Wilcox
Cover design by Rick/Simon
Photos on pages 22, 40, 48 and 60 from the Vancouver production of *Snowman* by Tim Matheson
Photos on pages 24, 55 and 67 from the Toronto production of *Snowman* by Guntar Kravis
Photos on pages 31, 39, 47 and 59 from the Montreal production of Snowman by Sara Mishara
Photos on pages 74, 79, 81, 84, 89, 98, 107, 115 and 117 from the Montreal production of girls! girls! girls! by Zoë Tousignant

Coach House Books
401 Huron Street (rear) on bpNichol Lane
Toronto, Ontario
M5S 2G5

416 979 2217
800 367 6360

mail@chbooks.com
www.chbooks.com